FOND DU LAC PUBLIC LIBRARY

32 SHEBOYGAN STREET

FOND DU LAC, WI 54935

WITH A LITTLE HELP
FROM MY FRIENDS

WITH A LITTLE HELP FROM MY FRIENDS

THE MAKING OF SGT. PEPPER

George Martin
WITH William Pearson

LITTLE, BROWN AND COMPANY
Boston   New York   Toronto   London

First U.S. Edition

ISBN 0-316-54783-2
Library of Congress Catalog Card Number 95-75251

10 9 8 7 6 5 4 3 2 1

MV-NY

Printed in the United States of America

CONTENTS

List of Illustrations   *vii*

Foreword   *xi*

Prologue   *I*

1. 'What do you see when you turn out the light?'   6

2. 24 November 1966: 'No one I think is in my tree . . .'   *13*

3. 'I don't really want to stop the show . . .'   *25*

4. 6 December 1966: 'Yours sincerely, wasting away . . .'   *34*

5. 'There, beneath the blue suburban skies . . .'   *39*

6. 19 January 1967: 'Well I just had to laugh . . .'   *50*

7. 1 February 1967: 'We hope you will enjoy the show . . .'   *63*

8. 8 February 1967: 'It's time for tea and meet the wife . . .'   *71*

9. 9 February 1967: 'And it really doesn't matter if I'm wrong I'm right . . .'   *85*

10. 17 February 1967: 'A splendid time is guaranteed for all . . .'   *89*

11. 23 February 1967: 'Where would I be without you?'   *95*

12. 28 February 1967: 'The girl with kaleidoscope eyes . . .'   *100*

13. 9 March 1967: 'A little better all the time . . .'   *107*

14. The Album Cover   *113*

15. 15 March 1967: 'With our love — we could save the world . . .'   *123*

16. 17 March 1967: 'Fun is the one thing that money can't buy . . .'   *133*

17. 'What do you see when you turn out the light?'   *141*

18. 'It's getting very near the end . . .'   *147*

19. 1 June 1967: 'Their production will be second to none . . .'   *151*

20. Epilogue: 'Life flows on within you and without you . . .'   *162*

Coda   *167*

Index   *169*

LIST OF
ILLUSTRATIONS

Between pages 52 and 53

1. *Beatles unplugged*
    As they were when I first met them, 1962
    (© Apple Corps Ltd)
2. *We've got a new drummer*
    The first real session, 1962
    (© Apple Corps Ltd)
3. *Brian with his 'boys'*
    (© Apple Corps Ltd)
4. *It goes like this*
    John plays me a new song
    (© Apple Corps Ltd)
5. *Head arrangement*
    George, Paul, John and their producer, 1963
    (© Apple Corps Ltd)
6. *Bigger than Jesus?*
    John explains, 1966
    (The Hulton-Deutsch Collection)
7. *The Heart of Liverpuddle*
    EMI's advertisement for the first single not to get to
    Number One on release
    (EMI Records)
8. *'Well, that's it, I'm not a Beatle any more'*
    The Beatles at the beginning of the *Sgt. Pepper* recording,
    1967
    (The Hulton-Deutsch Collection)
9. *A day in the life*
    Improvisation at 1.37 a.m.
    (© Apple Corps Ltd)

10. *With very little help from my friends*
    (© Apple Corps Ltd)
11. *Writer and producer seeing eye to eye*
    (© Apple/Beat Publications)
12. *Within me, without me*
    George in pensive mood
    (© Apple Corps Ltd)
13. John always liked a bit of brass
    (© Apple/Beat Publications)
14. *Inner light*
    John, George, Ringo, Patti Boyd with the Maharashi in
    Bangor, August 1967
    (© Apple Corps Ltd)
15. *There will be a show tonight . . .*
    The original Benefit for Mr Kite
    (Tom Hankey)
16. *The Fab Four with the Fab Four*
    The press launch of *Pepper* at Brian Epstein's house
    (The Hulton-Deutsch Collection)
17. On the sofa *chez* Epstein
    (The Hulton-Deutsch Collection)
18. *The great minds behind the album sleeve*
    (© Michael Cooper Collection)

Between pages 116 and 117

1. *Anyone at home?*
    Outside Brian's house in Chapel Street
    (© Jan Olufsen)
2. *We made it inside!*
    (© Apple Corps Ltd)
3. *Linda shoots Paul, 1967*
    (The Hulton-Deutsch Collection)
4. *Getting better all the time*
    The two Georges with Paul
    (© Apple Corps Ltd)

5. *No one I think is in my tree*
    John in the 'Strawberry Fields' video
6. *Except perhaps me*
    Paul in the 'Strawberry Fields' video
7. *All You Need Is Love . . .*
    (and a touch of genius)
    (The Hulton-Deutsch Collection)
8. *Just in case you don't understand plain English*
    The multinational live broadcast of 'All You Need Is Love'
    (The Hulton-Deutsch Collection)
9. *Where's the orchestra?*
    A run-through of 'All You Need Is Love'
    (The Hulton-Deutsch Collection)
10. George with his mentor, Ravi Shankar
    (© Apple Corps Ltd)
11. *A bit of hula*
    An early video after the release of *Sgt. Pepper*
    (The Hulton-Deutsch Collection)
12. *Mug shots*
    (Waldo Designs)
13. *Inflated Beatles*
    Some of the *Sgt. Pepper* merchandise
    (Waldo Designs)
14. *Fan fare*
    Sgt. Pepper keyrings and badges
    (Waldo Designs)
15. *A Colourful Record*
    A specially printed limited vinyl edition
    (Waldo Designs)

FOREWORD

Books about the Beatles must make such a big pile by now that there should probably be some sort of law against adding to it. Most of them have been written by people who poked, prodded, catalogued and criticized the Fab Four's story without actually being part of it. I've seen error in all of these accounts.

My own book may not be very much different, because I am relying on that most unreliable of servants, my memory. Someone once said that anyone who claimed to remember the Sixties couldn't actually have been there. I know exactly what he means. A lot of the written evidence I looked at is unreliable too: we all look at life through our different-coloured spectacles. So what follows is a personal view, based mostly on my personal memories.

A few years ago, I was up at AIR studios with Paul, and we were reminiscing like the old codgers we've become. Suddenly, we found ourselves disagreeing over a silly little detail. I said that George had done something, 'No, it was Ringo,' said Paul. We were both so sure of ourselves. Then we fell about laughing. 'My God!' I exclaimed, 'if we can't get it right, who the hell can?' Henry Ford was right when he said history is bunk. But then, as the song goes, 'it really doesn't matter if I'm wrong I'm right . . .'

There are many people I would like to thank. If anyone deserves the impossible title of 'Fifth Beatle', it is Neil Aspinall. Never in the limelight, Neil has served them faithfully from the very beginning, helping them in their complicated lives. I'd like to thank you for helping me steer my way through the sea of lawyers on both sides of the Atlantic when I was producing *The Making of Sgt. Pepper* for television in 1993.

This film was the starting point for *Summer of Love*. I am indebted to Rupert Perry, at EMI Records, for seeing the potential of a television programme which takes the viewer through the creative process of making a special Beatles album. Thanks also to my co-producer, Nick de Grunwald, for his patience and persistence, and for finding our director, Alan Benson, whose talented eye shaped *The Making of Sgt. Pepper* into a film that has won awards in many countries. Melvyn Bragg gave us his support just when it was needed, and guaranteed us a UK television slot on his excellent *South Bank Show*. The film would not have been made without the vision of Etienne de Villiers, President TV of Bueno Vista International. Etienne not only gave the project his blessing but persuaded the Disney Corporation in the US to back it.

Being strictly a DIY man in the heady world of literature, I brought *Summer of Love* to life in fits and starts. I owe thanks to Charles Armitage, then, for tactfully pointing out that it would, on the whole, be better if the book were published a reasonable time before my obituary notices. Many thanks to William Pearson, who cleverly jogged my memory with probing questions, and applied my nose to the grindstone alongside his so that the job got done. I also appreciated the help and guidance of our editor, Georgina Morley.

At Abbey Road, my old stamping ground, my friends Ken Townsend and Alan Rouse gave unstinting help and a great deal of their time, for which I am grateful. Mark Lewisohn was invaluable in helping to keep my memory on the straight and narrow. Thanks are also due to Ann Denvir and Tommy Hanley at Apple for their help with the illustrations and both William and I would like to thank Andy Davies and Richard Free for their help tracking down Beatles memorabilia.

Closer to home, my good friend and long-suffering assistant Shirley Burns gave me flattering encouragement, and I would have been in a real mess without the help of my dear wife Judy, who recalled and relived with me the ups and downs, the good days and the bad, and always made me laugh when I felt down.

Finally, many thanks and love to four fascinating, impossible, enormously talented, infuriating, adorable young men, who changed all our lives some thirty years ago.

This is their story.

PROLOGUE

It was the Summer of Love.

US Air Force B-52s were dropping 800 tons of bombs a day on North Vietnam; Mao Zedong's Red Guards had the whole of China by the throat; and Biafra's Ibo people were starving when they were not being massacred.

But from where I was sitting, at EMI's Abbey Road studios in west London, people in their thousands were giving themselves over to Peace and Love. They were dropping out, growing their hair, painting their bodies, and inventing sex. They contemplated revolution, and their navels. Flowers gave them power. They had pot and acid, optimism and enthusiasm. They had 'happenings', 'be-ins' and 'love-ins'. They had idealism, energy, money and youth. And they had one other thing. They had music.

The good vibrations kept on coming, from Hendrix and the Who, from Jagger and from Joplin, from Dylan and the Beach Boys and the Doors and Tamla Motown. In flats and bedsitters, peace-camps and parks, in huts and high-rises and apartments the world over: they were listening. From Rio to Rimini, Dallas to Djibouti – in their millions they turned on and tuned in.

On 1 June 1967 they heard the clarion call, the toppermost, poppermost sound of an entire generation.

It was a ground-breaking album by the Beatles. It was Hippy Symphony No.1. It was called *Sgt. Pepper's Lonely Hearts Club Band*.

And it was, after all, the Summer of Love.

Sgt. Pepper's Lonely Hearts Club Band was a musical fragmentation grenade, exploding with a force that is still being felt. It grabbed the world of pop music by the scruff of the neck, shook it hard, and left it to wander off, dizzy but wagging its tail. As well as changing the way pop music was viewed, it changed the entire nature of the recording game – for keeps. Nothing even remotely like *Pepper* had

1

been heard before. It came at a time when people were thirsty for something new, but still its newness caught them by surprise. It certainly caught me on the hop!

Pepper drove a splitting wedge through the heart of British pop; many see it as the watershed. By shutting themselves (and me) up in the studio for six months and doing their own thing, the Beatles put a question mark over what everyone else in the business was doing. The question was: are you making music, or just money? Do you blow musical bubble-gum, or play rock with a hard centre? Up until this point, the Beatles had been pretty much bubble-gum artists. With *Pepper*, they drew a line and crossed it.

The Beatles themselves never pretended they were creating art with *Sgt. Pepper*, or scrabbling after some kind of musical 'integrity'. They just wanted to do something different, and *Pepper* was it. Nowadays, when rock music in its turn has been commercially disembowelled, the distinction between the two forms of music is blurred. But it is still there, and *Pepper* caused it.

With *Sgt. Pepper* the Beatles held up a mirror to the world. And in this looking-glass the world saw a brilliant reflection of its kaleidoscopic 1967 self. It saw not the shambolic and often absurd cavortings of the hippy movement, but its perfect image – an elegant ideal; not the sordid gutterland of drug addiction, but the intriguing possibility of creative substance abuse.

Here, in any case, was a forty-minute vision one could trip to and have fun in. Pepperland was a place where friends helped you get by, traffic wardens came to tea, holes could be fixed and Mr. Kite guaranteed a splendid time for all. Things, in this never-never land, were getting better all the time.

This curious and wonderful album was more than a fanfare for the peace and love movement, though: much more. It had all kinds of other things in it that were definitely not bubble-gum. You might not notice that the lights had changed. It was so very strange: some of its songs seemed – well, profound. Whole chunks of the lyrics were completely unfathomable. People spent hours, days even, dissecting them. Journalists were paid good money to write about them. The Beatles seemed to be saying something, delivering a message that was never quite clear, no matter how many times we listened; and how we all listened!

'Within You Without You' – What on earth was that about? Was it even of earth? Wasn't it a mantra of the other-world, outside human time and space, ethereal, dreamily philosophical? It encapsulated the immemorial wisdom of the East, of the Vedic mysteries. It was out there pushing at the frontiers of the karma. This really was far out. This was wonderful. The Beatles were no longer writing catchy songs just to cheer people up – they had moved light years on from all that. They were mystics!

Pepper had even more up its brightly coloured sleeve. It was a special place, a dream-world in which we could all stumble across our perfect love, suddenly there at the turnstile, and be whisked off to nirvana in a newspaper taxi. It was an escapist fantasy. That was it.

Hang on a moment, though. Kaleidoscope eyes? Tangerine trees? Rocking horse people eating marshmallow pies? He blew his mind out in a car? We're talking psychedelia. Funny cigarettes? Lysergic acid diethylamide? Were the Beatles inviting us to join the reefer revolution, expand our tiny minds, and act like the sinister Doctor Leary? God forbid!

Mind-expansion. This was dangerous stuff. People might start to question things. We could be talking subversion. The Beatles were in fact political revolutionaries; they were abusing their power, that awesome power conferred by the adulation of the masses. They were undermining the state with their Peppery pernicious example, in the most insidious way of all – by means of music!

Wasn't that taking it much too seriously, though? Wasn't this album all really rather tongue-in-cheek, nothing more than the most talented pop group in history setting out its most wonderful ever stall? Wasn't it, then, just a harmless if occasionally satirical snapshot of a mixed-up crazy world? Yes, perhaps that was it. But then again . . .

Sgt. Pepper was, in short, all things to all people. The world looked into it and saw what it wanted to see. Like all really good pop music it reflected, in an unsystematic sort of way, its life and times. Yet many thought it was a precisely focused statement. There were as many 'interpretations' of its 'message' as there were people

3

willing to listen to it – and muse upon its cover. The BBC, at least, made its mind up straightaway: it banned 'A Day In The Life' the moment the album came out, on the grounds that it 'could be considered to have drug-taking implications'. The enormous kerfuffle on its release is a measure of the sheer and staggering diversity, the amazing many-headed flowering of the Beatles' talent that *Pepper* encapsulated.

What did this album mean, finally? Nobody knew for sure; no one could say. That was one of its greatest strengths – its almost total obscurity. People were convinced that it must add up to something. There was that cover, for one thing. Why put all those cultural icons on it, unless they meant something? Why print all the lyrics, for the first time ever on an album cover, unless the Beatles were making a statement? And then there was the endless ambiguity of the words. You could go on and on chewing them over for days, and be none the wiser.

Like its creators, *Pepper* was greater as a whole than as the sum of its parts. Individually, the tracks could be grappled with. In some cases they were quite straightforward. Together, though, they added up to something rich and strange – something that defied deconstruction.

Sgt. Pepper's Lonely Hearts Club Band expressed perfectly a feeling that was very much in the air at the time: that everything and anything was up for grabs. For a few short years the world had stepped back into adolescence. Life was an adventure playground, living to be toyed with. Cushioned by a climate of prosperity and pretty near full employment, young people had the space, the time and the income to indulge themselves in the endless experiment of self. If you couldn't make it in straight street (and who wanted to?), you could make it in 'counter-culture', fuelled on drugs, sex, Eastern philosophy and rock music. Weren't the Beatles living proof of this, and wasn't *Pepper* their flagship? They had shown in their music that you could, if you had a mind to, re-invent yourself endlessly and at will. So ... couldn't we all do it, if we gave ourselves enough space and time, freed our heads and maybe oiled the wheels a little with some pot? Well, couldn't we? *Sgt. Pepper* would give us the answers ...

The sixties, for me, was a love-in. – George Harrison,
South Bank Show

Pepper best articulated that great welling up of life and energy that swept over Britain in the sixties. The Beatles were in the vanguard of the Carnaby Street, Mary Quant, 'Swinging London' scene. The old order seemed to be crumbling, the new disorder riding high. Deference had gone out of fashion, irreverence, John Lennon-style, was in. Not everyone relished it, but the future had arrived with a bang. Everything was on the move. Art had gone pop. Aldrich and Truffaut, Polanski and Lumet, Chaplin and Antonioni – a feeding-frenzy of film-makers was in town, making a completely different kind of movie. Theatre exchanged the middle-class sofa for the working-class sink. Radio went through a similar revolution, revolting many in the process: pirate or official, Caroline or Radio One, the airwaves now vibrated to the manic beat of pop. Fashion was in overdrive: hemlines were the highest things in town, and that was saying something; manufacturers of Afghan coats went over to round-the-clock production. Chelsea's King's Road was a-glow with multicoloured mini-skirts, redolent with incense, a-rattle with love-beads, a-jangle with bells. Even the Queen's English was being tortured into accepting the new superlatives of a carefree age: 'gear', 'hip', 'fab', 'with-it', 'swinging', 'groovy', 'where it's at'.

England, in those days, was where it was at. And it was pop music that helped keep this bright fire burning. Every week, every day, almost, from about 1963, a fantastic new group or singer hit the scene; not just any old group knocking out any old sound, but the likes of the Kinks, the Rolling Stones, Procol Harum and the Who. 'A Whiter Shade Of Pale', 'Like A Rolling Stone', 'My Generation', 'House Of The Rising Sun', '(I Can't Get No) Satisfaction' . . . That was the kind of thing we were hearing for the first time, quite apart from any of the Beatles' songs – or the wonderful stuff coming out of the United States. Imagine what that was like.

CHAPTER ONE

'What do you see when you turn out the light?'

By 1966 the Beatles were in a car that was going downhill very fast. This is not to say that their career was going downhill; but they were a media juggernaut that was increasingly out of their manager Brian Epstein's control – and everyone else's, for that matter. It wasn't so much that somebody was pressing the accelerator too hard; it was that nobody had their foot on the brake.

Offers for them to appear were winging in daily from every corner of the world. Brian kept on accepting future dates, never thinking that 'the boys' were being subjected to too much pressure. He loved the helter-skelter of wheeling and dealing, the juggling of countries and dates, the hot kick of power. Managing the Beatles made him important, and respected by all.

At the end of 1966, Brian was forced to face up to something he had never dreamed he would have to confront: that the Beatles would refuse to perform live again. He had signed them for five years, in 1962, to do just that: get out there and knock the world for six. He fully expected them to go on doing it for another five years, and five more after that. Without any warning, though, they were climbing down from the stage, and turning their backs on it for ever. They just said, 'No,' to his concert dates, and went on saying it. Going by the received wisdom of the day, this amounted to commercial suicide. Many groups at the time did no recording at all, relying entirely on live performances for their success. The idea that the Beatles wanted to stop performing and spend months recording an album – *Sgt. Pepper* – shook Brian terribly. He thought it was the end.

Brian saw himself as a latter-day Diaghilev, as an impresario of great international acclaim, the master of an empire of which the

Beatles were a prominent part – but only a part. He never saw himself as simply the servant to the greatest group ever. Even so, what would or could be the role of this media Napoleon if his greatest asset no longer needed managing?

There was no doubt that the year 1966 had been a disaster for the Beatles. The world was caving in on them. Newton's First Law, that for any given action there is an equal and opposite reaction, had come into play. The universal hysteria the Beatles had inspired was producing its inevitable kickback.

In June, while they were appearing in Hamburg, they received an anonymous telegram. 'Do not go to Tokyo,' it said. 'Your life is in danger.' We all took the threat seriously, not least because there was so much religious and conservative opposition in Japan to the forthcoming concerts. The venue was to be the Nippon Budokan Hall, which many Japanese held sacred: certainly not the place for profane Western pop music, anyway. The Japanese police took the death threat very seriously indeed, so that the tour took place in a state of siege, broken only by furious armour-plated rushes to the concert hall.

The Beatles' next stop, Manila, was scarier still. Ferdinand and Imelda Marcos ruled the Philippines like medieval despots. People did what they said, or else. When Brian received a 'suggestion' that the Beatles pay a courtesy call on the First Lady on the way to their afternoon concert, he should have considered it carefully. But the band had been playing in Europe immediately before heading for the Philippines, and after a long journey they were not too happy about an official visit to the Marcos family on their only day off. They asked Brian to explain to Marcos that the visit would not be possible for them in the time available and to ensure that they were given plenty of notice. They added that their days of rest were too rare to be filled with official events like this. Brian sent a telegram to the promoters and to the Palace. The only response was something like, 'They must come nevertheless. The offer cannot be refused.' Once the boys had arrived in Manila it was obvious that there was a big problem.

Paul has since told me that Brian and officials from the Palace begged the Beatles to reconsider, but they stood their ground. After all, they had given them plenty of notice. They reckoned that the attitude of the Filipinos – ignoring their polite declining of an invitation – was cavalier in the extreme. The Beatles never liked being bullied – it would only stiffen their resolve. A military escort arrived at the hotel to take the group to Malacanang Palace, and Brian had to choose between the wrath of the Beatles or the President of the Philippines. It says a lot for his courage that, despite an armed contingent at the door, he refused to wake the boys – sound asleep in their beds.

They could hardly have done anything worse to wound the national pride, let alone the feelings of Imelda Marcos, who had invited scores of her aristocratic cronies along with their children for a private view of the Famous Four. Brian found out just how much trouble they were in when he switched on the television between the two planned shows.

The whole country was up in arms. Although the concerts had been immensely successful, it seemed every Filipino was out for their blood. Everything was done to make their departure as uncomfortable as possible. It was extremely unpleasant. One of the party, their driver Alf Bicknell, stupid enough to shake his fist at someone, was actually pushed down a flight of stairs. Tony Barrow, the Beatles' publicist at that time, was recalled to the terminal to deal with many hassles, while Brian and the boys tried to make themselves as inconspicuous as possible behind a group of handily placed nuns. It seemed the best bet at the time! Barrow returned with the news that they were to be taxed for the entire fee that they had earned. Neil Aspinall and Mal Evans, following behind Brian and the Beatles, were looking after all the luggage and gear and found suddenly that the escalators were out of order. Mysteriously they started up again after they had lugged everything up the stairs. The next port of call was India, but guess where all their luggage ended up? Sweden! The Beatles came away from the Philippines with no money, no luggage, but with a lot of headaches and expense!

A bad summer, which got worse in August. Masters of public relations until then, the Fab Four had always handled the press pack with a combination of wit and wisdom, charming the pants off most reporters. Then it all went horribly wrong. In March, John had given an unguarded interview to Maureen Cleave, a prominent

London journalist. Published in the *London Evening Standard*, his comments included the fateful words, 'Christianity will go. It will vanish and shrink. I needn't argue with that; I'm right and I will be proved right. We're more popular than Jesus now. I don't know which will go first – rock 'n' roll or Christianity.'

Five months later, the front cover of the US teen magazine *Datebook* ran a banner headline quoting John's pessimistic view of organized religion. Result: mayhem. Although it was probably true that congregations in Christian churches had been dwindling since the war, the mention of Jesus Christ in the same sentence as the Beatles was nothing short of heresy. It brought the world down around their ears, and with good reason. No fewer than twenty-two US radio stations banned Beatles songs from their playing schedules. Piles of Beatles books, music and memorabilia went up in smoke, with organized bonfires in some cases broadcast live. The Bible Belt called for condign punishment. And all this was happening on the very eve of a US tour.

Brian Epstein flew to the States to try to limit the damage. What could be done to rescue the situation? There was nothing for it but John would have to apologize. At first he flatly refused the humiliation, but when it became clear that the success of the tour depended on it, he gave in and said he was sorry. Even so, the tour, which began in Chicago on 12 August 1966, was a very uneasy one. Some tickets for the Shea Stadium performance even had to be given away. This was incredible to Brian, as it was to me. It was the only time we could remember when the band had played to anything less than a full house.

Brian's main fear on that last tour, like my own, was for the physical well-being of the Beatles. Even in 1964, with no overt threats to their safety, we had worried about this. Before their concert at the Red Rocks Stadium in Denver, Colorado, Brian and I climbed up one of the giant lighting towers that straddled the stage. From our bird's-eye vantage point the auditorium spread before us, a vast natural amphitheatre. A cold feeling spread through my stomach. I looked across at Brian. From the look on his face, I could see the same thought had occurred to him: a sniper could pick off any one of them at will. John F. Kennedy's assassination the previous year had made us realize that such horrors were all too possible. In 1967, in the wake of John

Lennon's incautious remarks, they seemed all too probable.

As if all this were not bad enough, the Beatles, when they did tour, were no longer even able to hear themselves sing and play, on stage, for the screaming. This was perhaps the worst thing of all. The Beatles were, first and foremost, musicians. This is easy to forget; their fame tends to obscure the fact, as does the apparent ease with which they wrote and performed their material. They themselves were acutely aware that a succession of routine concerts in deafening surroundings was affecting their musicianship. It was depressing to them.

They also had a bad case of hotel fatigue. The boys were tiring of their prison of fame, and each wanted his own identity back. Being a Beatle had been a lot of fun, despite the recent setbacks. But that was what you were, twenty-four hours a day, seven days a week: a Beatle. There was no time set aside to climb off the merry-go-round, to be Richard Starkey again, or George Harrison. You went to bed with a scream in your ears, and you woke up the next morning to the same shriek.

> **No, we were absolutely fed up with touring, and why were we fed up with touring, because we were turning into such bad musicians. The volume of the audience was always greater than the volume of the band. For me personally, there was no chance I could do a fill, because it would just disappear. So I ended up just sort of hanging on to the other guys' bums and trying to lip-read to see where we were.**
>
> – Ringo, *South Bank Show*

I don't believe that those who have not done it themselves could understand the pressures of life on tour. It sounds marvellous being a multi-millionaire pop star, having the whole world at your feet. In actual fact it is a lot of hell. Even in the most comfortable hotel you are a prisoner. Being inside the New York Plaza, with several thousand screaming fans outside, is like being in Alcatraz – only the room service is slightly better.

> **... there was one show where even I broke, which was rain-sodden, and the rain was in the amps ... we**

had just a little bit of tarpaulin over the thing and it was really unpleasant to play ... I remember we all used to run into the back of these big vans they'd hired, and this one was like a silver-lined van, chromium, nothing in it, like a furniture van with nothing in it, just chrome; we were all piled into this after this really miserable gig, and I said, 'Right, that's it, I agree with you now ... between the four of us let's give the gigging up ...' — Paul, *South Bank Show*

It had been tough on Brian, too, that year. As soon as he got back to England he went down with glandular fever. When he was well enough my wife Judy and I joined him for a much-needed weekend of rest, relaxation and strategic discussion at Portmeirion in North Wales, the curious seaside hideaway built like some giant film set by the architect Clough Williams Ellis.

As he took stock, Brian came to realize that he had taken a great deal for granted in running the lives of his four famous charges. So far, they hadn't complained about the gruelling round of concerts and appearances he put them through. Nor did they mutter about the exhaustion they experienced when Brian, unused to American distances, would schedule them for successive nights in cities that were sometimes literally a thousand miles apart. Their disenchantment in the autumn of 1966 was more a reaction to public and press hostility in the wake of John's Jesus Christ gaffe; to the death threats they had received in Hamburg; to the violence they had found in the Philippines; and to the general awfulness of their half-unpacked-suitcase life-style.

Well that's it, I'm not a Beatle any more.
— George Harrison, on the plane home to London after the
Candlestick Park concert in San Francisco

One has to put all this doom and gloom in perspective. To most people in the world of 1966, certainly in Britain, and to an overwhelming extent in America, the Beatles were still the absolute tops. Prince and pauper alike hung on their musical, and indeed other pronouncements; monarchs queued up for the favour of their presence. Their most banal remarks were elevated to the status of profundity – their more serious, as in the case of John's off-the-cuff remarks about Jesus, could result in mass bonfires of Beatles records and the attentions of the Ku Klux Klan.

What they said and did mattered – absolutely. That was the measure of their importance.

Even in the early years of Beatlemania, grown men, grown, sober businessmen, were wearing Beatle wigs to work along the streets of New York, and would greet one another at nine o'clock in the morning with, 'Say, who are you today? I'm George Harrison . . .' 'Yeah, great! I'm Ringo . . .' Looking back, this is hard to believe – but I saw it.

In 1964, in the USA, you could tune right across the frequency spectrum of a transistor radio, station after station, and hear nothing at all over the airwaves but that one sound – the Beatles. Three years down the road from that, they were untouchably, unreachably, unforgettably the greatest.

They had climbed to the top of the mountain; now they were looking curiously around them. It was time to take stock, to get back to their first and most constant love: making music.

CHAPTER TWO

24 November 1966: 'No one I think is in my tree . . .'

It is impossible for me to talk about *Sgt. Pepper* without mentioning two crucial songs that neatly bracket it: 'Strawberry Fields Forever' and 'All You Need Is Love'. If 'All You Need Is Love' says everything about where the Beatles were in terms of popularity and success, 'Strawberry Fields Forever' shows us where they were musically. Destined originally to be on *Pepper*, it set the agenda for the whole album.

I am not sure how much cold-blooded analysis has to do with one's passion for a work of art. It is a bit like falling in love. Do we really care if there is the odd wrinkle here or there? The power to move people, to tears or laughter, to violence or sympathy, is the strongest attribute that any art can have. In this respect, music is the prime mover: its call on the emotions is the most direct of all the arts.

An initial gut reaction to a piece of music is almost always right. When I first heard 'Strawberry Fields Forever', I was thrilled. When I hear it now, it can still send a shiver along my spine.

I heard it first on a cold windy night in November 1966. We were in Abbey Road's Studio No. 2. John was standing in front of me, his acoustic guitar at the ready. This was his usual way of showing me a new song – another of my extremely privileged private performances . . . 'It's goes something like this, George,' he said, with a nonchalance that concealed his ingrained diffidence about his voice. Then he began strumming gently.

A couple of introductory chords, and we were straight into that starry, echoing line: 'Living is easy with eyes closed . . .' That wonderfully distinctive voice had a slight tremor, a unique nasal quality that gave his song poignancy, almost a feeling of luminescence. I was spellbound. I was in love.

'What do you reckon?' asked John, quite nervously, once he had come to a stop. John was never one for too much praise. But he could tell that I really liked the song even before I spoke. Lamely I replied, 'It's great, John. That's a really great song. How do you want to do it?'

'I thought you were supposed to tell me that!' he flipped back at me, laughing. In truth, I wish now that I *had* told him; I would have taken the song just as I heard it. Oh, how I wish I had caught that very first run-through on tape and released it!

'Strawberry Fields Forever' was gentle, dreamy, uncharacteristic of John then. He had broken through into different territory, to a place I did not really recognize from his past songs. There had been a hint of it, perhaps, in 'Tomorrow Never Knows'. But this!

John composed 'Strawberry Fields Forever' in Spain. He had a small part in the Richard Lester film *How I Won the War* as one Private Gripweed, and it came to him during the endless breaks between takes on the set. The song has all the languorous, sun-flowery heaviness of a Spanish summer afternoon in it, despite being a memory-capsule of a childhood in the north of England.

If this was the measure of things to come, we would have a superb album. It was completely unlike anything we had done before. It was dreamlike without being fey, weird without being pretentious. In strong contrast to the solid realism of 'Penny Lane', which Paul wrote immediately after it, 'Strawberry Fields Forever' wrapped its nostalgia in an aura of mystery, conjuring up a hazy impressionistic idyllic dream-world.

In fact, 'Strawberry Fields' was the name of a Salvation Army hostel in Liverpool not far from John's childhood home. In reality the place was hardly the stuff of romance, but in John's song it became a kind of heaven. The very words 'Strawberry Fields' evoke a summery meadow in shimmery warm sunshine, where you can drift and dream in a wonderful limbo.

Studio 2

It was all done very clinically, that's the joke. We were in this big white room that was very dirty and hadn't been painted for years, and it had all these old sound baffles hanging down that were all dirty

and broken. There was this huge big hanging light, there was no window, no daylight. It was a very clinical, not very nice atmosphere. When you think of the songs that were made in that studio it's amazing, because there was no atmosphere in there, we had to make the atmosphere. After a number of years we asked them could we have some coloured lights or a dimmer or something like that; after asking them for about three years, they finally brought in this big steel stand with a couple of red and blue neon lamps on it. That was the magic lighting they gave us.

The refrigerator had a padlock on it, so if we wanted a cup of tea we'd have to break open the padlock on the fridge to get the milk out. We had to do that every night for five years, it wasn't like they realized, Oh well, they drink tea after six o'clock, so we'll leave the fridge open, oh no, they padlocked it, all the time. It was weird.

– George Harrison, *South Bank Show*

John's other world, the one in his mind, was always and for ever the world he preferred to live in. It was a far more comfortable place to be. The real world somehow never quite matched up to his expectations. As he put it: 'It's getting hard to be someone, but it all works out . . . It doesn't matter much to me.'

The brilliance of the song's lyrics lies in the way they call up strong images, using the often illogical and disjointed language of everyday speech. Play back a tape of people talking, and you hear words used out of context, sentences in reverse order, interruptions, 'ums' and 'ers' and hesitations all over the place. The spoken word is a shambles. Listen again to John's song, and you will hear this exquisitely captured: 'Always no sometimes think it's me, but you know and I know it's a dream . . .'

Who else could get away with a line like that?

John's music was a perfect complement to his ingeniously distorted verse. As in so many of his songs, much of the melody in the verse of 'Strawberry Fields Forever' is based around one note, with shifting, quicksand harmonies underneath giving it grip. This melodic interweaving is the key to the whole song: it sparked off

15

its unforgettable instrumental introduction, and allowed John's voice to linger and dwell on its plaintive monotone.

The song's form was also pretty unusual: a verse and short chorus only, with no middle eight. The chorus changes the mood, making a more definite statement. The sudden change of the harmony, placing stress on the 'to' of 'Where I'm going *to*' has a dramatic impact that I am sure was not calculated, but the product of sheer instinctive musical genius.

How to begin recording such a song? John's one idea on the arrangement was to use the mellotron, his favourite toy of the moment. The mellotron was a Heath Robinson contraption if ever there was one; you could virtually see the bits of string and rubber holding it together. It was as if a Neanderthal piano had impregnated a primitive electronic keyboard, and they'd named their deformed, dwarfish offspring 'Mellotron'. (The Musician's Union tried to ban this contraption, on the grounds that it would 'kill' live music; I reckoned it was more likely to kill the operator!)

It played taped recordings of real instruments, on a loop of tape that sounded when you pressed one of the limited number of keys. This tape was about seven feet long, and was drawn across a playback head by an electric motor until its length was used up – whereupon a strong spring snapped it back to the beginning again. This meant that if you held down a note longer than a couple of seconds, the machine would give a loud hiccup and stop while it rewound and reset itself. You learned to play fairly short notes!

Another designed-in drawback was that the tape speed was hardly ever consistent, so 'wow' as we call it nowadays was common, and the pitch was always a little suspect. There was a master speed control knob which, when twiddled, gave infinite pitch variation of up to about a fourth – five or six semitones. The mellotron was also very large and monstrously heavy, squatting in a polished wooden cabinet rather like a horizontal wardrobe.

We began recording 'Strawberry Fields Forever' in Studio No. 2 of EMI's Abbey Road complex on Thursday, 24 November 1966. No arrangement had been written for the song; the four Beatles sat down to work it out in the studio as they went along. John had sketched out the basic structure: 'We'll start straight in with the verse, no intro, follow with the chorus, then back for another verse, and so on.' Right, John.

John wanted to keep his acoustic guitar for this session, so Paul took over on the mellotron. With Ringo on drums and George on electric guitar, the song was heavier-sounding that I had imagined it from my initial run-through with John, but it came together very quickly. Almost immediately, we arrived at a take that we thought would be the final one. That first take is brilliant, especially John's vocal: clear, pure, and riveting. As he sang it that night, the song became hypnotic: gentle and wistful, but very strong too, his sparse vocal standing in sharp contrast to the full sound of George's electric guitar, Paul's imaginative mellotron and Ringo's magnificent drums.

Sticking to John's original idea, 'Strawberry Fields Forever' started with what became, in the finished version, the chorus: 'Living is easy with eyes closed . . .' (The introduction that we all now know had not yet been written.) Typically, John asked for a speed change on his vocal recording. I thought his voice was one of the all-time greats, but he was always asking me to distort or bend it in some way, to 'improve' it, as he thought. So when we overdubbed his vocal, we pumped up the tape frequency to 53 hertz instead of the normal 50 hertz. On playback at normal speed the change lowered his voice by a semitone, making it sound warmer and huskier.

It was a magical evening. We all loved the beginning to our new album, and went home in the early hours of the next morning, Friday, tired but satisfied.

Over that weekend, however, fertile imaginations went to work, and by the time we arrived for the session on Monday it was obvious that John and Paul had come up with plenty of ideas on how to improve 'Strawberry Fields Forever'. I had thought our baby was perfect, but . . .

I had long ago drummed into them how important it was to get to the nub of a song as early as possible. This was what John wanted to do now, by starting on the chorus: 'Let me take you down . . .' instead of 'Living is easy with eyes closed . . .' as it did before.

It was a good move, because the lyric now immediately seized you by the throat. The song made you share an intriguing journey, instead of beginning with an abstract comment. It was as if John was grabbing people in off the street, to go with him to a party. But it did still need an introduction. Paul had been doodling around

17

with the chords of the verse, and he turned up a sequence of notes which were really the song's chords, but stretched in an arpeggio style.

This simple but inspired piece of composition made a brilliant introduction to John's song.

Imagine our four-track tape. I had the option of making only four distinct recordings on to it, and I had to be careful how to ration them. We earmarked Track 1 for drums, but we couldn't afford the luxury of having just one instrument on that track. Ringo had to share his sounds with Paul on the mellotron, and George playing maracas. Ringo made the drumming sparser than on our first recording, using his tom-toms to punctuate the song more effectively.

Track 2 at this stage had George playing his electric guitar finger-picking style, which created a melodic counterpoint to the lyrics. On Track 3 we overdubbed Paul's bass, with John taking the opportunity to add a few judicious downward swoops on the mellotron, using his beloved speed control knob. As the song grew, my excitement grew with it. It was really turning into something. Finally we put down a main vocal track from John, before packing up for the night at around 1.30 a.m.

Still we were not finished. We were excited on this one. At 2.30 the next day – really early for us – we were back. We recorded another take, Take 6, following pretty much the shape of the previous day's Take 4, then dubbed this on to a new four-track tape to give us a couple of extra tracks. The new tape, with a few more vocal and instrumental frills on it, was numbered Take 7, and there we had it: the 'Strawberry Fields Forever' master.

We were all elated, and we left the studios early, at about eight in the evening, after completing a mono mix of what I took to be the finished song. The boys each took home an acetate demo of our re-mix.

There was just one small thing: John came to me a week later and said he still wasn't entirely happy with what we had done. The song kept eluding him: he could hear what he wanted, in his head, but he couldn't make it real. We had never re-made a song from scratch before, as he now wanted to do. But I was as determined to get to the truth of 'Strawberry Fields Forever', to the sound John knew was there inside him, struggling to get out, as he was himself. What would he do with it?

His suggestion surprised me: I still had that early simplicity in mind. But he wanted to use strings and brass, and would I score them for him?

We arranged a recording session for the following Thursday, 8 December, to lay down the new rhythm track. The boys wanted to come in at 7 p.m. There was only one small snag: I had promised to attend the première of Cliff Richard's new film, *Finders Keepers*, that evening. Geoff Emerick, our engineer, was invited along too. We decided to risk it and attend the première: quite often the Beatles would turn up late – or sometimes not even at all. That night they turned up bang on seven o'clock. Such is the law of Sod.

When Geoff and I strolled in at about eleven, Studio No. 2 was in the grip of a controlled riot. The boys had decided it would be fun to lay down an 'unusual' rhythm track for 'Strawberry Fields Forever' on their own, with anyone and everyone available simply banging away on whatever came to hand. The racket as we walked in was like something from a very bad Tarzan movie. John and Paul were bashing bongo drums, George was on huge kettledrums, joined sporadically by Paul; Neil Aspinall was playing a gourd scraper, Mal Evans a tambourine, and George's friend Terry Doran was shaking maracas. Someone else was tinkling away on finger-cymbals. Above it all, Ringo was struggling manfully to keep the cacophony together with his regular drum-kit. The Beatles were at play, and here was I coming in to party-poop!

Towards the end of this rogue track, which Dave Harries, as stand-in engineer, was doing his best to record, everyone was whooping or yelling, and John can clearly be heard chanting very slowly, and in time to the rough-and-ready beat: 'Cranberry sauce, cranberry sauce . . . ' Why cranberry sauce? Why not? It was coming up to Christmas!

Some of that wild and whacky recording survived through to

the release of the record, and you can still hear John chanting these words, if you listen closely. This gave rise to one of those absurd Beatle myths: that Paul was dead. Instead of 'Cranberry sauce', people heard 'I buried Paul' – or thought that was what they heard. (In 1969, in the US, an imaginative DJ invented the myth that Paul was dead. It spread like a bushfire in a strong wind. All sorts of other 'evidence' was cited in support of this fiction, including the fact that Paul had his back turned to the camera on the back of the *Pepper* sleeve, and of course those famous bare feet on the zebra-crossing cover photograph of *Abbey Road*, later on. Madness!)

A few years earlier, George Harrison had stumbled on a sitar while he was wandering around a set of the film *Help!*. George's subsequent research into Indian music bore luscious fruit on our next stab at 'Strawberry Fields Forever'. He brought in a swordmandel – a sort of North Indian table-harp. The only way he knew how to play it was to stroke it as you would a real harp, so he spent ages tuning it to produce the right selection of notes. His patience rewarded us well, because the glissando he charmed out of the instrument was tremendous, adding a fantastically good effect when we dropped it into our rhythm track. John discovered a way of making the mellotron play not just one but a whole random sequence of notes, which gives 'Strawberry Fields Forever' another marvellous touch of madness towards the end. Paul then came up with an inspired piece of ringing lead guitar work that rounded the song off brilliantly.

Meanwhile I still had to organize the instrumental accompaniment John had requested. I booked in four trumpet players and three cellists for overdubbing on 15 December. I believe in economy in music – not to save money, but to get a clarity that using too many instruments will sometimes cloud. I had less than a week to write the score that John was looking for. I knew he wanted the brass to be bright and punchy, but I felt the chords needed a bit of reinforcement on some of the changes.

Having a basic recorded track to write to was a great advantage. It meant I could see where to put the flesh on the bones. I decided the cellos should speak with one voice, in unison, forming a bass counterpoint to the melody. The trumpets I wrote either in simple triad (i.e. three-finger) chords, or with a unison staccato emphasis, blasting away on one note.

I confess I had heard a lot of American records with very groovy horn sections by this time, and lifted one or two ideas from them. As the song developed further it seemed natural to use the trumpets as a harmony behind the voice, sounding the same phrase as in our lovely intro. Then came the only section I had qualms about. At this particular point the tempo is held together by a fast rhythm from a cymbal that Ringo recorded backwards – never an easy sound to latch on to. The cellos worked against this urgent beat with a slower, triplet time motif, and I was not at all sure that it was going to work. But now, I am happy to say, I cannot imagine the song without it.

Recording the parts I had written was very difficult to get exactly right: all four trumpets had to play loud punchy spiky stabs in perfect time, while the cello parts demanded equally accurate and strident bowing. They had to fit our frenetic rhythm track to perfection, which I found to be virtually impossible. I had quite forgotten that our kindergarten rhythm play-in inevitably did not conform to a rigid quartz-controlled beat. The tempo was all over the place.

Musicians today take it for granted that if they are overdubbing, their basic track never varies in its tempo; but our rhythm track would vary even from one bar to another! It was not much out of time, but enough to make life hell if you were trying to fit something to it. Having said all that, I believe that Ringo's drumming on this song is some of his best. His quirky figures accented it in exactly the right way from the outset, complementing John's phrases beautifully throughout all the changes the song underwent.

Mixing a four-track master really should not be too difficult. These days, with forty-eight tracks as the norm, mixing becomes as much of a performance as the original recording, and it can take longer. But with four tracks, basic balances have already been achieved in the recording and dubbing processes. We had been mixing our chosen best tracks as we went along. With all the variations that 'Strawberry Fields Forever' had thrown up, though, John could not make up his mind which of our performances he preferred. He had long since dismissed the original statement of the song on Take 1, and was now torn between the slow, contemplative version and the frantic, percussive powerhouse, cello and brass arrangement of Take 20.

21

Ever the idealist, and completely without regard for practical problems, John said to me, 'I like them both. Why don't we join them together? You could start with Take 7 and move to Take 20 halfway through to get the grandstand finish.'

'Brilliant!' I replied. 'There are only two things wrong with that: the takes are in completely different keys, a whole tone apart; and they have wildly different tempos. Other than that, there should be no problem!' John smiled at my sarcasm with the tolerance of a grown-up placating a child. 'Well, George,' he said laconically, 'I'm sure you can fix it, can't you?' whereupon he turned on his heel and walked away. I looked over at Geoff Emerick and groaned.

Every time I go on about the primitive state of recording technology in the mid-sixties, I feel like Baron von Richthofen describing the Fokker Triplane to a group of Concorde pilots. But it must be said that nothing on the technology front existed, at EMI's Abbey Road studios anyway, that could help us out of this fix. There was no way those two performances could be matched. Unless . . . unless . . . I realized that because Take 20, the frenetic take, was faster – much faster – I could try slowing the tape right down. This would not only bring down the tempo, it would lower the pitch. Would it work? A whole tone was one hell of a drop . . . almost twelve per cent; but it had to be worth trying.

We called up our magnificent band of backroom boys, who wheeled in a Diplodocus-sized washing machine lookalike: the 'frequency changer'. This valve-powered monster – a lash-up devised by Ken Townsend, our Chief Engineer, and his merry men – took the mains electricity supply, and bent the alternating current up and down on either side of the normal fifty cycles per second. Don't ask me how they did it, I haven't a clue. What I can tell you is that it used to get very hot, and would explode in a shower of sparks if you stretched it too far. But it was all we had. We hooked it up. We were looking for a point in the song where there was a sound change, which would help us disguise the edit of the century. We found it precisely one minute in.

That edit has always stuck out like a sore thumb for me, but nobody else seemed to notice. John was obviously pleased with the result and accepted it as the finished song, but it was no more than he expected. The extremely difficult he thought of as par for the course; only with the utterly impossible were you allowed to take more time. Once he had an idea, it had to be captured quickly. If it did not materialize in very short order, he tended to wander off and lose interest.

The way we worked, the creative process we always went through, reminds me of a film I once saw of Picasso at work, painting on a ground-glass screen. A camera photographed his brushwork from behind the screen, so that the paint appeared as if by magic. Using time-lapse photography you could see first his original construction, then the complete change as he applied the next layer of paint, then the whole thing revitalized again as he added here, took away there. It reached a point where you thought, 'That's wonderful, for heaven's sake stop!' But he didn't, he went on, and on. Eventually he laid down his brush, satisfied. Or was he? I wonder how many of his paintings he would have wanted to do again. It was a fascinating film of a great artist, of a brilliant creative mind at work. And I have often thought how similar his method of painting was to our way of recording. We, too, would add and subtract, overlaying and underscoring within the limitations of our primitive four-track tape.

There were many things we abandoned or taped over: the first take of 'Strawberry Fields Forever' is a good example. It was great, but we ditched it outright. It could be greater still. Then there is the end section of the orchestrated version of the song, where the rhythm is too loose to use. In spite of all our editing, I just could not get a unified take with complete synchronicity throughout. The obvious answer would have been to fade out the take before the beat goes haywire. But that would have meant discarding one of my favourite bits, which included some great trumpet and guitar playing, as well as the magical random mellotronic note-waterfall John had come up with. It was a section brimming with energy, and I was determined to keep it.

We did the only thing possible – we faded the song right out just before the point where the rhythm goes to pieces, so the listener would think it was all over, then gradually faded it back up again, bringing back our glorious finale. It was our own little bit of Picasso technique, a dab on the canvas that we managed to rub out, leaving behind an exotic touch of colour . . .

There are many cases of Beatles records I can think of where we could have kept it a bit more simple, where we might have overdone it; but 'Strawberry Fields Forever' is not one of them. Way ahead of its time, strong, complicated both in concept and execution, highly original and quickly labelled 'psychedelic', 'Strawberry Fields Forever' was the work of an undoubted genius. We could not have produced a better prototype for the future. The care and attention we lavished on that track, its technical and musical excellence, John's readiness to throw away a good but unsatisfactory take and re-make – these things set the pattern for what was to become *Sgt. Pepper's Lonely Hearts Club Band*. We were all very proud of our new baby. For my money, it was the most original and inventive track to date in pop music.

The Beatles no longer had the millstone of madcap live performance tours around their necks. Now that they had some time and space, they were spreading their musical wings. They were showing us what they could really do.

Many years later John and I were sitting in the kitchen of his apartment in the Dakota building in New York, mulling over past glories like a pair of old codgers. John suddenly looked up at me. 'You know what, George,' he said. 'If I had the chance, I'd record everything we did again.'

'What?' I replied. 'Even "Strawberry Fields Forever"?'

'Especially "Strawberry Fields Forever",' he said. 'Most of what the Beatles did was rubbish.' It shocked me. For John, the vision was always better than the reality. Everything inside him was greater than its expression in the outside world. That was his life.

The only true songs I wrote were 'Help!' and 'Strawberry Fields'.
                                                    – John Lennon Remembers

CHAPTER THREE

'I don't really want to stop the show . . .'

If ever there was a case of somebody needing someone else, back in the spring of 1962, it was Brian Epstein and myself. He needed me: and, boy, did I need him.

Brian and I always worked very closely together. We would have an overall plan of when we wanted records to come out, and we would also work out carefully the dates for the Beatles' recording sessions. After *Revolver* hit the shelves in August 1966, the Beatles were scheduled to come back to Abbey Road at the end of the year to make a new album.

We did not know what it was going to be; it was simply part of the process that had become established by then – four singles and two albums a year – an astonishing schedule by today's standards. From nowhere, though, the Beatles had decided to throw away the rule-book. The big question now was, would anything of that cosy old recording and sales routine survive? Could we even count on a new album in 1967 at all?

Knowing that they were tired of the goldfish bowl, knowing that the American market had faltered slightly, did nothing to help Brian get a grip of a very fluid situation. All he could see was that the Beatles were refusing to come out and play any more. They were going to shut themselves up in the studio, perhaps for months! Brian saw the black pit of obscurity yawning before him. And there was the 1966 Christmas market to take care of; we had to have something strong for that. It was with a tinge of panic in his voice, therefore, that Brian came to me and said, 'We need a single out, George, fast. What have you got? I want the best thing you've got.' He was determined to make up any lost ground, to keep the Beatles firmly in the limelight's brilliant blaze.

What I had got was a small collection of gems. By this time, we had already completed three brand-new titles: 'When I'm Sixty-Four', 'Strawberry Fields Forever', and 'Penny Lane'. We were working on 'Good Morning, Good Morning', and 'A Day In The Life'. What about that for a choice!

Realizing how desperate Brian was feeling, I decided to give him a super-strong combination, a double-punch that could not fail, an unbeatable linking of two all-time great songs: 'Strawberry Fields Forever' and 'Penny Lane'. These songs would, I told him, make a fantastic double-A-sided disc – better even than our other double-A-sided triumphs, 'Day Tripper'/'We Can Work It Out', and 'Eleanor Rigby'/'Yellow Submarine'.

It was the biggest mistake of my professional life.

Releasing either song coupled with 'When I'm Sixty-Four' would have been by far the better decision, but at the time I couldn't see it.

The all-important music charts were run by the three music papers: *Melody Maker*, *New Musical Express*, and *Record Mirror*. These rival charts were compiled from a fairly crude system of record retailer reports, submitted by different outlets each week. If I had stopped to think for more than about a second, I would have realized that one great title would fight another; and this is exactly what happened. The reports came in, and they showed that our double-A-side was selling extremely well. There was only one problem. The weekly sales figures showed that *two* singles, 'Strawberry Fields Forever' and 'Penny Lane', were selling well. They were being counted separately! As far as the charts were concerned, one side was effectively cancelling out the success of the other.

I firmly believe that if the total sales of those two sides had been added together we would have squashed the opposition flat. As it was, a sentimental old-fashioned ballad called 'Release Me', by a new singer with the unlikely name of Englebert Humperdinck, was outstripping us. For the first time since 'Please Please Me' in 1963, the Beatles did not make it to the number one spot in the charts with a new single.

It broke the roll: we'd had twelve successive number ones. It had become as reliable as the sun coming up – and we took it almost as much for granted. Alas, with unlucky number thirteen, it was not to be. Despite being the best singles they had ever, in my opinion, released, the double-A-side stalled at number two in the *NME* charts, even though the combined sales got bigger and bigger. This little contretemps did not restore Brian's flagging morale.

From the outset, Brian and I had been determined to give the buying public good value for money. We had agreed that if a song had been released as a hit single, we should try not to use it as a cynical sales-getter on a subsequent album. To our way of thinking, this was asking people to pay twice for the same material. I know it seems ludicrous these days: now a hit single is frequently used to sell a whole album; but we thought differently then. This was why 'Strawberry Fields Forever' and 'Penny Lane' did not make it on to *Sgt. Pepper* as originally intended.

It was not really like Brian, that panic over the 1966 Christmas single. Until that autumn his faith in the Beatles had been almost religious in its fervour. It was this steamroller conviction that had swayed me crucially when we first met, on that February day in 1962, when the future of the group hung by a hair.

He was a Liverpudlian record store manager with strange dreams, at his wits' end flogging a dead horse called the Beatles. I was running EMI's smallest label, a comedy, light entertainment and jazz outfit called Parlophone. He was entirely new to the game; I had been recording since 1950. We were both getting a bit desperate.

Short of setting fire to himself in the foyer of Decca Records, Brian had done everything he possibly could to kick-start the Beatles' recording career. Decca had firmly rejected the Fab Four that year, judging their sound distinctly unfabulous after auditioning them. Columbia, HMV, Pye and every other label he had approached with the Beatles' demo tape had turned them down – including the Woolworth's Embassy label – without even the courtesy of an audition. The doors to fame and fortune were proving very hard to push open. It was beginning to look as though he would have to slink back to minding the family shop, reneging on those starry promises to his 'boys' of dizzying fame and fortune.

Wriggling on the hook of impending failure, Brian made one last stop at the HMV music store on London's Oxford Street. Doggedly, he decided to get an acetate disc made of the Beatles' demo tape, just in case something should turn up. He was a kind of musical Mr Micawber, was Brian Epstein. Except that for Brian something did turn up.

I did.

So much, though, was down to pure chance. The engineer making the transfer in the HMV shop listened to the raucous racket blasting out at him and decided it was quite good. Different, anyway. His name was Jim Foy. 'Have you taken this anywhere?' he asked Brian. 'I mean, to any of the recording companies?' 'Everywhere,' said Brian, 'and they all said the same thing: "No."'

'Have you tried a music publisher?' asked Foy. 'No,' replied Brian. 'Tell you what,' said the helpful engineer. 'Why don't I give Syd Coleman a ring? He's right here, on the top floor. He might be interested.' Picking up the telephone, Jim duly rang Syd. And with this simple act he set in train a sequence of events that would turn the world of pop music inside out.

A few minutes later, a slightly bemused Brian found himself being ushered into the well-carpeted presence of the head of Ardmore & Beechwood, the EMI music publishing company. The two men exchanged formalities.

'Who have you seen, Mr Epstein?' began Syd.

'Pretty well everyone,' Brian admitted, trying hard not to sound too sheepish.

'And you want to publish this group's music, is that it?'

'No,' replied Brian. 'I want to get them a recording contract.'

'Have you seen people at EMI?' asked Syd.

'Yes.'

'EMI have turned you down? Phillips have turned you down, and Pye?'

'Yes,' said Brian, gritting his teeth. 'We did a test for Decca, but they turned us down, too.'

'Well,' said Syd, 'have you tried Parlophone?' Brian looked back at him blankly. 'Who's Parlophone?' he asked.

'A guy called George Martin,' replied Syd. 'He makes comedy records. He's had a big success with the most unlikely recording acts.'

'Good Lord,' thought Brian, 'I've really hit the bottom now.'

Syd called me up on the spot. 'George,' he said, 'I don't know if you'd be interested, but there's a chap here who's come in with a tape of a group he runs. They haven't got a recording contract, and I wonder if you'd like to see him and listen to what he's got?'

'Certainly,' I replied. 'I'm willing to listen to anything. Ask him to come and see me.'

'OK, I'll do that. His name's Brian Epstein.'

When I said that I was willing to listen to anything, it was absolutely true. Comedy records were all very well; they had even begun to put Parlophone on the map. But I was looking, with increasing desperation, for an act from the pop world.

There were four EMI labels working out of Abbey Road in those days: HMV, Columbia, Parlophone and Regal Zonophone. Columbia had the CBS catalogue: Frank Sinatra, Doris Day, Guy Mitchell . . . HMV had all the RCA Victor imports from the USA: Elvis Presley, Harry Belafonte, and so on. These two labels were the big time. Regal Zonophone, and my own outfit, Parlophone, were very small beer in comparison. The producers at HMV and Columbia had, as we know, already shown Brian the door. He was well acquainted with EMI's Abbey Road studios – from the outside.

Despite this, Brian gamely turned up to see me at the appointed hour. By this time I had graduated to Oscar Preuss's old office, where the reception desk now is. It was Oscar who had given me my first big break into recording, head-hunting me back in 1950 to be his assistant, when I was in a lowly clerking job at the BBC Music Library in Great Portland Street.

Oscar had retired, and I had taken over not only his office, but his young and beautiful secretary, Judy Lockhart Smith. The first thing she did when I arrived in my new guise as the boss was offer to resign – an offer I hastily refused, since she was the person who held things together at Abbey Road. It was as well for me that she stayed – ten years later we were married.

When he turned up for our appointment that day, Brian Epstein struck me as an amiable, engaging young man, with the heart and liver of a born entrepreneur. He was well spoken, exceedingly smart in his astrakhan coat with its velvet revers. He put his precious piece of newly minted acetate on to the turntable. We listened.

The quality of the recording was appalling. Not only that, but these Beatles, as they called themselves, were grinding out a succession of ballads that were beginning to sound mouldy even then:

things like 'Over The Rainbow', or 'Besame Mucho', interspersed with the odd blues classic, like Fats Waller's 'Your Feet's Too Big'.

In common with most of the British recording industry at the time, Brian firmly believed that a well-crooned ballad was the guaranteed and indeed only route to success. So he had insisted the Beatles record that type of song for their demo tape. After all, he argued, the charts were full of it, so it must be what people wanted. Instantly, though, it seemed to me that the sound the Beatles were making, their whole style of singing and playing, was completely unsuited to that sort of material. I began to get a little fidgety.

But wait a minute . . . In among all the creaky crooning, the band members had worked up a couple of their own tunes. The songs they had written were called 'Please Please Me', and 'Love Me Do'.

When the demo was finished I switched off the machine and looked at him. 'It's not great,' I said. 'I don't really know . . .' While I dithered, Brian launched forth into his sales pitch, praising the Beatles to the skies. 'One day,' he told me, with a fanatical glitter in his eye, 'they'll be bigger than Elvis Presley.'

While he was getting this panegyric off his chest, I was thinking hard. I was looking for something. What I was looking for was my very own Cliff Richard. I had always been very envious of Norrie Paramor, one of my colleagues at Abbey Road. It was so easy for him. He produced Cliff for the Columbia label, and very well, too. Meanwhile, here was I flogging my guts out recording Bernard Cribbins and Charlie Drake and Rolf Harris, trying to find songs that would fit them, that were funny and would sell. It was hard work. What's more, each record was a one-off; whereas with Cliff Richard all you had to do was give him a half-decent song to record and he had a hit. Would the Beatles turn out to be my Golden Goose? I doubted it. Still, there was something there I couldn't quite put my finger on, something interesting – and, at the very least, it was new.

'Tell you what,' I said. 'The only way I can decide is to meet them. Bring them down to London, and I'll take them into the studio and test them.'

According to the received wisdom, they arrived for their audition at EMI Abbey Road on 6 June 1962, just after completing their latest Hamburg tour. Not knowing what sort of recording sound they were expecting from me, I called them into the studio. 'Come and have a listen to what we've got,' I said, 'and tell me if there's anything you don't like.' George Harrison's gun-slinging reply, 'Well I don't like your tie, for a start,' is a hoary old chestnut of Beatles lore, now. I wouldn't be forgetting these guys in a hurry, whatever happened.

They ran through their set, which was much as I had heard on the demo acetate – rough, and not very ready. There was something else about them, though, quite apart from their music, that was immediately obvious on meeting them: they had the magic ingredient – charisma. They exuded exuberance. Sparks flew off them while they were playing, as well as when you talked to them one-to-one. Individually and collectively, these four very young men had an overwhelming irreverent charm. No one could have resisted their warmth, their wit and their quick-fire repartee.

Their experiences in the seamy nether world of Hamburg night-life had helped them to learn how to work and hold an audience. They had massive stage presence. If the average beer-sodden crowd on the Reeperbahn didn't like what you were doing on stage, it was liable to stand up as one and throw a few chairs at your head. The four boys in front of me had learned to be engaging, the hard way.

I began to see what Mr Epstein had been getting excited about. I did not find myself reaching for a chair. But I did want to stand up, if only to applaud. There had to be a market for all that star quality, but where was it?

All the time they were playing, I was thinking, 'Which one's the best looking? Who's got the best voice?' I was looking for a new Buddy Holly and the Crickets, for a new Cliff Richard and the Shadows. I didn't see them as a group. Would it be Paul McCartney and the Beatles, or John Lennon and the Beatles? It had to be one or other of those two, that much was obvious. Pete Best was extremely handsome, in a moody, James Dean-ish sort of way, but he was the least outgoing – and his drumming . . . I wasn't sure. Though they all shone brightly in their own ways, John and Paul were the stars.

Then they played 'Love Me Do'. Although Lennon and McCartney had written it together, I had asked Paul to sing lead because I wanted John's harmonica part to bleed into the vocals. He obviously couldn't sing and play at the same time. So Paul was warbling away and John was backing him with that peculiarly distinctive, nasal, almost flat second harmony that was to become a trademark of their early sound. And it suddenly hit me, right between the eyes. This was a group I was listening to. I should take them as a group, and make them as a group. That distinctive harmony, that unique blend of sound – that was the selling point. It was that 'something' I had dimly recognized from the demo lacquers. I could not think of any other group or sound in pop music like it, even among the dozens of US imports I had listened to. There were echoes there of the Everly Brothers and the old blues heroes, of Elvis Presley and Chuck Berry, but there was also something entirely new, something English, something that was Liverpool, something Beatles. The 64,000-dollar question was, would it sell?

There was only one way to find out. I signed them. The meanness of that first Beatles contract has passed into legend: but I signed them. (Legendary meanness was company policy and I was to discover it didn't apply only to the artists. EMI never paid me a bonus, despite having a number one record for thirty-seven weeks. In 1965, I tried to renegotiate my contract. I discovered that Parlophone had made EMI a profit of £2,200,000. And I saw none of it – even under the new terms they were offering. So I defected in August that year and set up AIR, Associated Independent Recording, leasing myself back to EMI to produce the Beatles and others – and to make some money.)

Keen-eyed Beatles fans will have noticed that I am rewriting the official history of the group. I signed the Beatles on 4 June 1962: the original contract still exists with that date on it. I would never, ever, have offered a contract to Brian Epstein for a group I had not met, or heard live. Yet most versions of events state that the first Beatles audition – and thus our first meeting – did not take place until 6 June. But this, according to the contract, was *two days* after I had signed the group for three years!

I don't think it was quite like that. My memory is of a recording audition in No.3 studio, at EMI Abbey Road (the upstairs studio), in *March* 1962. This memory is backed up by my wife, Judy Lockhart Smith. If this is true (and it makes much more sense from my point of view), it means that the initial meeting between Brian and myself did not take place on 9 May, but three months before that. I liked what I heard at that first, previously unremembered, audition sufficiently to offer Brian Epstein a recording contract. This is why he sent his telegram of 9 May informing the Beatles that he had secured a contract for them to record 'for EMI on Parlaphone [sic] label.' This was not a mad rush of enthusiasm to the head, following our (supposedly) initial chat, on 9 May, as has been suggested – it was simple fact. I raised an 'Application for Artiste' contract with the office on 18 May, which was duly signed on 4 June. Meanwhile, on 27 March, Brian wrote to Bert Kaempfert, who had the Beatles under contract until 30 June 1962, asking him to release them from that contract. It is worth quoting some of Brian's letter: 'As it happens, the particular recording Company *with whom we have negotiated* (my italics) are unable to record the group until they return from Germany, and in any event prefer to wait until their existing contract with yourself has expired.' That's my version of events, so it must be true!

CHAPTER FOUR

6 December 1966:
'Yours sincerely, wasting away . . .'

Deprived as we now were of two beautiful tracks with the single release of 'Strawberry Fields Forever' and 'Penny Lane', the first song that we did earmark for use on the new album was 'When I'm Sixty-Four'. This, on the face of it, was a whimsical, music-hall number, the sort that Paul loved to do from time to time, and very straightforward to record. The song had been lurking around in Paul's mind for a long, long time, ever since I first knew him. In fact, when the group's amplifiers broke down in the Cavern club, as they frequently did, the Beatles used to fill in the gap while repairs were being done by knocking out this song, among others, with acoustic guitar backing.

I am sure Paul wrote 'When I'm Sixty-Four' with his father in mind. Paul's father had played in a dance band in the post-war years. It so happened that Jim McCartney was sixty-four years old in July 1966. Jim loved music-hall stuff, corny popular songs, the kind of thing that Paul normally wouldn't tolerate. Nevertheless, 'When I'm Sixty-Four' was not a send-up but a kind of nostalgic, if ever-so-slightly satirical tribute to his dad.

On one level, I am sure it was an echo of the songs Jim played when Paul was young. It's almost a Des O'Connor number. It is also not really much of a Beatles song, in that the other Beatles did not have much to do on it.

Paul got some way round the lurking schmaltz factor by suggesting we use clarinets on the recording, 'in a classical way'. So the main accompaniment is the two clarinets and a bass clarinet, which I scored for him. This classical treatment gave added bite to the song, a formality that pushed it firmly towards satire. Without that, the song could have been misinterpreted – it was very tongue-in-cheek. It is rather like, say, putting a Gerald Scarfe cartoon into a gilded frame, and hanging it in the National Gallery. The form brings you up short, makes you think more carefully about the content.

We began the recording on 6 December 1966, with Paul singing a guide vocal and accompanying himself on bass guitar, while Ringo played brushes on snare drum. All that went on to Track 1. (You would never dream of putting a vocal on the same track as the drums today, because you can never separate them afterwards. These days, with multi-track recording, you keep every element isolated, so you can fiddle about with it all at will.)

On Track 2 we overdubbed a piano line from Paul, and on Track 3 we had Ringo's brushes and snare again, allowing me to get rid of the original drum take, the one with the voice on it. That was all we did that day. Two days later, Paul sang a 'proper' vocal on to that basic track of 'When I'm Sixty-Four'.

We did no more to the song until 21 December. I'd already mixed the four tracks we had from the first couple of days' work down on to Track 1 of a fresh four-track tape. Then we overdubbed two clarinets and a bass clarinet on to Track 2, played by the best clarinet players you could get in the business then: Robert Burns, Henry MacKenzie and Frank Reidy. We added Ringo playing chimes on to Track 3, together with vocal harmonies from Paul, George and John. All George and John had contributed to the song, at that point, were these backing vocals.

Track 4 took another recording of Paul's voice. We originally recorded him in the key of C major; but when it came to mixing, Paul wanted to sound younger. Could he be a teenager again? So we racked up his vocal to D flat, by speeding the tape up. His vocal sounded thinner and higher: not quite a seven-stone weakling, but nearly. The recording was complete!

The arrangement of this song is deceptively simple, but in a way it underlines my constant belief in simplicity in orchestration. By restricting ourselves to three instruments only (two clarinets and a bass clarinet) we could hardly be lush. Every note played had to be there for a purpose. 'Indicate precisely what you mean to say,' was a line that summed up Paul's thoughts on arranging, too. Paul always knew clearly in his own mind exactly how he wanted the song to sound. I encouraged Paul to develop his natural talent for arranging, and at one stage he took lessons in music theory. I think he found learning and sticking to the rules harder than he had expected. He also worried about inhibition, not wanting the straitjacket of musical discipline to block his free inspiration, rightly enough.

One of the last, and unusual, additions to 'When I'm Sixty-Four' was the sound of chimes. Abbey Road studios always had a collection of percussion instruments lying around, and Ringo could not stop himself having a go at them.

Most people think of 'When I'm Sixty-Four' as a jokey song, a piece of tongue-in-cheek music-hall pastiche, which it is. Nor did the other Beatles take the song terribly seriously. The Beatles historian Mark Lewisohn describes it, accurately enough in so far as it goes, as 'Paul's vaudeville-style charmer'.

For my money, though, it has a little more to it than that. The song is also a horror story: Paul's personal vision of hell. In those days, the four Beatles were unable to imagine themselves growing old. Paul, as he told me, couldn't really believe it would happen to him.

Lots of us have this attitude to old age when we are young. The idea of being even forty years old is inconceivable, too horrible to contemplate. In the sixties it was a particular sin to be old and alive. In 1962 Paul said, 'When I reach the age of forty I won't be playing songs like "Love Me Do"!' John, on the other hand, said poignantly a few years later, 'When I'm sixty-four I hope Yoko and I are a nice old couple living off the coast of Ireland, or something like that – looking at our scrapbook of madness.' For John, so sadly, it didn't happen. Paul is now over fifty and continues defiantly to tour the world, dispensing extraordinarily accurate versions of his great Beatles songs to massive and frantically appreciative audiences. And he will probably go on doing it for some time to come.

If you look at the lyrics you can see that underneath the jokiness they are saying, 'Isn't old age awful? Banality, tedium, nothingness, poverty, routine.' It is Paul with his satirical tin hat on, a bit like, in film terms, *Oh What a Lovely War*. The bleak underlying vision is dressed up in this very gentle, rooty-tooty kind of charm.

To be young in that heady dawn was bliss indeed, to steal a thought from Wordsworth. Most young people took a happy, secure life completely for granted. The relative prosperity and full employment we enjoyed in the sixties helped. If you are worried about where your next crust is coming from, you are much less likely to experiment with alternative styles of living. As it was, in 1967, the younger generation was confident enough of its income to live a little. They were free to experiment with their lives; and how they experimented!

To be old, on the other hand, was very death. What was the point of being old? It meant you were missing one of the best times to be young in the history of the world so far! As for me, I was one of those who had missed this particular love-boat. I was regarded as very old indeed by the Beatles, although in 1967 I was only forty-one.

Paul's song brought back strongly memories of my own childhood. I do remember having some weird ideas around the age of five. As an infant I went one step further even than Paul, being convinced that growing up must be a fairy story in itself. I couldn't accept the idea that children ever turned into grown-ups. As for grandparents, that particular form of life had nothing at all to do with the joy of being as I understood it.

I remember my grandmother as a gigantic pyramid of human flesh – not that I ever saw any of it, since she was invariably draped in a voluminous black tent that stretched from her neck to the floor. She must have weighed a good 300 pounds. I never saw her feet, and often wondered, as a small child, whether she actually had any. Perhaps she was on castors, like one of the Daleks in *Doctor Who*? Her brother, my Uncle Fitz, was equally imposing: always in a three-piece suit, his ample belly decorated with a watch and chain of gleaming gold. He smoked cigars continuously, and you always knew when Uncle Fitz was around by the lingering smell of fine Havanas.

Grandma was bigger than her husband, but Granddad made up for his relative lack of bulk with an enormous walrus moustache. At mealtimes I would gaze at him in fascination, unable to take my eyes off his quivering drooping broom as he manoeuvred his soup and veg majestically past it. The thought that I might one day metamorphose into one of these three aged and very curious creatures myself was patently absurd. They belonged on another planet altogether, and I knew as a child I could never become anything like them.

But I've been caught out. The years have rolled by and are trying to catch up with me. On my birthday in 1991 Paul and Linda McCartney sent me a superb bottle of claret, an '83 Château Margaux. A little note attached to it said simply: 'Birthday greetings, bottle of wine.' It was a very kind thought, but he was a year out: I am even older! I was sixty-four the year before, in 1990.

That is the strange thing about time; it is the same no matter where you view it from. I believe I'm really the same person inside as that five-year-old with stupid ideas about grown-ups. I'm damned if I'm going to be a full-time oldster like my grandparents. In fact over the past six months I've been trying to retire: I've converted a London church into a vast, state-of-the-art recording complex; done a three-month world tour of Japan, Sweden and Brazil; recorded *Tommy on Broadway* with Roger Daltry and an album of George Gershwin songs with people like Elton John, Lisa Stanfield and Elvis Costello; oh, and written this book. I'm not going to 'grow old gracefully': I refuse!

When I heard 'When I'm Sixty-Four' for the first time, I chuckled at the cleverness of the lyrics. They were so true. They reflected my own experience of family life, the comfort and cosiness, so well. Nowadays, in a world of increasingly high-tech everything, I think that ordinariness is very important.

The song then, showed the other side of the Beatle coin on *Pepper*: it was not psychedelic, mystic, transcendental or any of those other things that have been levelled at the rest of the album. It was an affectionate satire regarding old age from a young man's point of view.

CHAPTER FIVE

'There, beneath the blue suburban skies ...'

We were all listening to Sleepy John Estes in Art School...
—John Lennon Remembers

By the time the Beatles came to record *Pepper* they had worked through, and to some extent worked out, the early influences that had helped to shape their music. But those influences were still important: a kind of background musical radiation. They are many and various, and some have already been written about at length.

The influence of Bob Dylan, for example, is obvious: 'Subterranean Homesick Blues', released in April 1965, was definitely not a song about mindless teenage love; its chainsaw lyrics and the striking film that went with it had a profound effect on the pop world, not least on the Beatles. But there is an influence on the Beatles that has not been chewed over quite so much, and that is the blues.

The blues are the true origin of rock 'n' roll. You can trace the blues back as far as you like, to the acoustic down-home/country blues of the American Deep South, to field holler, or even further if you care to. You would probably end up in West Africa, or on the slaving ships a couple of hundred years ago, with the captives singing about their hellish conditions.

The term 'blues' encompasses a sprawling range of musical styles. These are dangerous waters, but I am still going to stick my toe in – even at the risk of having it snapped off.

During the 'Great Depression' of the early 1930s, wave upon wave of impoverished and jobless black migrants from the southern United States moved to the northern cities, in particular to New York, Detroit and Chicago. These mushrooming modern conglomerations proved fertile ground for the music of oppression. The country blues musicians who were part of this mass move pretty soon discovered the electric guitar, transforming the old country blues tradition into something else entirely. Some have called this new sound the 'urban electric blues'. For modern white artists like the Beatles, it was this citified, later version of blues music that really got them going.

Many white artists, the Rolling Stones, for example, or the Yardbirds, took this electrified, twelve-bar blues form over wholesale and recreated it for a new, mainly white audience – an audience entirely ignorant of the original sound.* Elvis Presley began his career this way. So, too, did Jimi Hendrix. The Beatles used twelve-bar blues, but you will not find many Beatles compositions that have the twelve-bar blues as a basis. 'Matchbox', recorded by the Beatles in 1964, is an obvious example of one they did lift. It was first recorded in 1927 by one of the godfathers of the blues, Blind Lemon Jefferson. 'Can't Buy Me Love' (1964) and some other early Beatles compositions owe their structure to the twelve-bar

*Most readers will already know what I mean by the term 'twelve bar blues', but just in case there are any who might like a word or two of explanation . . .

In twelve-bar blues there is a sequence, constantly repeated, of twelve bars of common time. But the chords (usually three) follow a pretty rigid pattern within that sequence.

Evolving as it did from the early jazz of the Deep South of the United States, when the harmonies were driven by the piano player (backed up by a banjo), this form of music took on a new dimension with the development of the electric guitar. The music of Jelly Roll Morton and the boogie-woogie bass gave way to the real blues guitar players, like Hubert Sumlin.

In any given key, the chords revolved around the tonic, the dominant, and the sub-dominant. In plainer language, this means around the root chords of the first, the fifth and the fourth notes.

On a keyboard, then, playing in the key of C, the twelve-bar blues sequence would be as follows:

C C C C7   F F C C   G F C C

Sometimes the last bar would be G instead of C. You will notice a seventh added to the C chord on the fourth bar. Almost any chord could have a seventh in the sequence, and in the melody line the third would often be flattened; so in the sequence above, one could easily hear an E flat note in the melody, even though there would be an E natural in the C chord below.

This, then, is the twelve-bar blues, the basis of a great deal of jazz and pop music. Obviously there are exceptions, ('St Louis Blues' is one), but the number of popular songs that derive from this basic form is as unto the stars of heaven.

form. On the whole, though, the Beatles took the blues idiom, instead – the poetry in the music, its soul – and ran with that.

People say that Liverpool was the fount for the new music that shook Britain in the 1960s because the city had always been one of Britain's main Atlantic ports. Any records or music that came in via ships from the United States arrived on Merseyside first. In this analysis, you could trace the modern popularity of blues and country and western music on Merseyside back to the cotton ships that plied between southern United States ports (like New Orleans) and Liverpool during the nineteenth century and on into our own. Most of the cotton mills were in Lancashire; so it made all kinds of good sense to import the raw cotton through Liverpool. Maybe it is King Cotton that we have partly to thank for the rich and complex music of the Beatles.

There might just be another, more modern reason, though, why John Lennon was listening to Sleepy John Estes at a Liverpool art school in the 1950s. I would lay a tidy sum of money that Sleepy John was virtually unheard of anywhere else in the UK at that time. He isn't exactly a household name today. Why should Liverpool have been any different?

During the Second World War, the Atlantic convoys bringing very badly needed supplies and troops to this country from the United States aimed for the safety of the nearest landfall on the north-west coast of England: again, Liverpool. Convoys needed to reach port as quickly as possible. The fearsome toll in ships and lives taken by the wolf-packs of German U-boats made the twin towers of the Liver Building the sweetest thing an allied mariner could see.

It wasn't just ships that needed landfall, though: aircraft were pretty glad to reach terra firma, too, after flying three thousand miles over the briny. And thousands of them made the flight to an airbase, a few miles to the north-east of Liverpool: RAF Burtonwood. This base grew incredibly quickly in size during the early months of the war, until it was home to no fewer than 18,000 American military personnel – the biggest single site for US forces in Britain during the war. RAF Burtonwood was so big it became known as 'Little America'. Little America was the main entry point for anything and everything to do with the US Air Force in the European Theatre of Operations: bombs, rockets, aircraft spares, vehicles, men and women, all came through this installation, as did the aircraft themselves: B-24 Liberators, B-17 Superfortresses, P-51 Mustangs, P-38 Lightnings . . . Billy Graham preached there, Vera Lynn sang morale-building songs there, and General Dwight D. Eisenhower drew up his D-Day invasion plans there.

The base served the whole of the US 8th Air Force during the war, as well as the US 9th Air Force from 1944. It was what you might call a big-time operation. Thousands of GIs, white and black ('overpaid, oversexed and over here'), were brought in through Liverpool docks during the run-up to the D-Day landings of 1944.

What, I hear you ask, has any of this got to do with the music of the Beatles? Well, where there were US airbases or army barracks, there were US servicemen and women listening to US music. And many of these personnel were black. With them the doughboys/girls brought their culture – and their favourite records – plugging both directly into the mainstream of Liverpool life. The American troops certainly mingled with the local civilians when they were out on the spree in the Mersey area and Liverpool, with its docks, was an absolute magnet for them.

As for the local civilians, 'Little America' was in its turn an absolute magnet for any woman between the ages of fifteen and thirty. Girls flocked to it from the surrounding area, not just from Warrington, Liverpool and Manchester, but from even farther afield – Stockport, for example, sent regular contingents to the base dances, where American musicians would perform. Nylon stockings, chocolate, money, fun, and a dependable supply of attractive young men dispensing these things; no wonder they came. Many of these women – some 6500, in fact! – ended up crossing the pond when the airmen went back, as 'GI brides'.

I like the theory, anyway. There has to be some reason for the fact that Liverpool, of all British cities, actually had a vibrant teenage culture centred around pop music in the 1950s, when the rest of Britain was snoozing gently away in the pullovered arms of croon.

The Beatles, come to think of it, were Liverpool teenagers in the fifties. Now there's a thing.

Blues music mattered to the Beatles because of the directness of the songs, their underlying earthiness and emotion. They were songs about sex, about love, about poverty, about travelling without hope or money, and about the happiness to be had in life despite tough times. The songs had the 'real gone spirit'.

Instrumentally, the Beatles loved the loudness, the rawness of the guitar work, the heavy back beat, the thumping drums and bass, the fact that you could shout your head off when you were singing. Then there was the ubiquitous use of the harmonica. This ancient Delta and hillbilly instrument had somehow survived the blues' climb out of the Mississippi swamp, and John Lennon in particular loved it.

Dozens of great black artists – Muddy Waters, Howlin' Wolf, Sonny Boy Williamson, John Lee Hooker, Otis Spann – laid the musical groundwork for this rich inheritance. Of course, I had nothing to do with introducing the boys to any of this exciting stuff – they had already done that for themselves – but I knew enough to recognize those influences in their music, because of Parlophone.

One of my jobs at Parlophone had been to vet a whole stream of records for possible issue on that label during the 1950s. Most of these came to us from the King label, in the United States. An arduous job, that – listening for a living; listening to some of the best music ever pressed on to vinyl. Funnily enough, I hardly recognized my luck at the time.

King was a small R&B label, which had, like Chess, Vee Jay, Atlantic and Sun records, seen the musical worth and commercial potential of music by black artists. It started life as a 'race' label, described at the time as 'a label that records music by black people for black people'.

Some great unknowns like Nina Simone came my way via King – it didn't take much wit to add her to the Parlophone catalogue. But in terms of the Beatles, I particularly remember the records of Sonny Terry and Brownie McGhee, whose blues vocals and guitar had a haunting harmonica accompaniment. It was their rough-edged, down-home sound that immediately sprang into my mind that first sunny afternoon when John Lennon produced his 'harp', as he called his battered old tin harmonica, and started wailing away on it.

It was probably that harmonica sound that made me choose 'Love Me Do' as the first ever Beatles record. None of the songs I had heard from them, whether their own compositions or cover versions of standards, struck me as an immediate hit. But I thought the use of the harmonica on this new, bouncy, jangly, up-beat song was really original. It was certainly an unusual sound to be coming from white boys playing British pop music.

Blues music had a pretty small market in the UK during the 1950s. Britain had a relatively small black population at that time, and what there was of it tended to listen to reggae or jazz, being of West Indian origin. White people listened to jazz and pop. So blues music was a minority interest. I certainly did not take much notice of it, other than to decide what might sell on Parlophone. But among those who did listen, and avidly, were some of the new British bands springing up: the Beatles, and, most notably among the artists who followed immediately in their wake, the Rolling Stones.

As far as the UK labels were concerned, blues music tended to be lumped in with jazz, partly because British jazz musicians had done a lot to introduce it to these shores. Parlophone was very much a jazz label then; I was recording people like Humphrey Littleton, Jack Parnell, Johnny Dankworth, Freddy Randall & His Dixieland Band. The blues stuff I was hearing from King Records was much more raw, but as far as I was concerned, it was American black jazz. I thought it would have a useful hard-core following, and that would be the end of it.

The Beatles looked on this music in an entirely different way: as anything but jazz. In fact they looked on it almost as an antidote to jazz. What they listened to most keenly, of course, because it was closer to them in time, was the music of Chuck Berry and Co. This, for them, was the cutting edge of the blues.

Berry brought all kinds of influences to bear in his music, influences from cowboy music, from country and western, from gospel music and hillbilly folk. He concocted his very own, very modern-sounding mix. Berry took the urban electric blues sound, threw in everything else that he felt like, speeded it up, and increased the volume of everything massively – guitars, vocals, drums, the lot, insisting particularly on the backbeat. He created a brand-new guitar style. A disc jockey called Alan Freed coined a phrase to describe the new sound: he called it 'rock 'n' roll'.

This is what the Beatles seized on, the modified blues music of Chuck Berry, and of those who held on to his coattails, rather than what I have heard called 'pure Blues'. Berry and his counterparts made a sound that was very impolite, as different as could be from the genteel sound that British pop singers were making then. It was music that hit you in the guts, and, being young men, the Beatles liked to be hit in the guts. (I didn't. I was an old man, and still content to listen to the pap!) They took in this music, without trying consciously to imitate it, and used it as a springboard for their own musical invention.

In the early days of the Cavern, in the late 1950s, the Beatles (known at that time as the Quarry Men) were content to copy the early rock 'n' roll artists. But very soon they were taking this material as a jumping-off point, as the basis on which to write something that was uniquely their own. Taking a leaf from Chuck Berry's hybrid book, they swirled everything around in their own little Liverpuddle, and then exported it back across the Atlantic to the Americans, who happily accepted it as something new. And it was new.

The Beatles used to play me some of these records when we first met: the new, mostly black American rock 'n' roll records. When I first came across them their favourite artists were Chuck Berry, Carl Perkins, Bo Diddley, Jerry Lee Lewis, Fats Domino, Little Richard, Smokey Robinson, Roy Orbison, Buddy Holly and, of course, Elvis Presley. 'Have a listen to this!' they would say. 'Don't you think that's great?' I would not hear what they heard, but I heard something that was interesting and good.

By then I had been a record producer for so long that whenever I listened to anything new I was not listening only to the music: I was listening to the way the recording had been made, technically. What amazed me about the King label records, and the music the Beatles played me, was the sheer technical ferocity of the stuff. The US studios managed to pack so much volume on to a disc, much more than we could over here in the UK. I could pick up the newly imported piece of 45 rpm vinyl, look at it, and actually see the ear-splitting loudness of the record before I had even put it on. It was, as they say, in the groove.

'God,' I would say to them, 'why can't we cut a record like that?' If we had tried to cut a record as loud as that, the needle, probably the whole playing-arm of your Dansette record player would have jumped straight off the vinyl and fallen on the floor. But the American records didn't make the needle jump. They were technically streets ahead of us, and they could make these records that didn't just shout – they roared. I didn't know how they did it. But I wanted to find out, all right.

Nowadays getting massive volume on a track is simply a matter of pushing up a fader; in those days it was a real problem. The louder you could make that type of pop record, the more impact it was likely to have, and of course the better it was likely to sell. A disc jockey would put on one of these roaring records, and it would knock his socks off. You, the listener, would hear it over the radio for the first time, and it would knock your socks off. Out you would go to the record store and buy it. That's the business.

Getting maximum volume out of those grooves became my major preoccupation. I used to wake up in the middle of the night, thinking about it. Volume! That great sound . . .! I did succeed in getting some of that loudness into the early Beatles records, but I wanted more, much more. And the boys were snapping at my heels. They could hear the difference in the US imports just as well as I could. 'Why can't we get it like that, George?' they would chorus. 'We want it like that!'

Well, why couldn't I get it like that? It was because of things like cutting the bass sound on to a disc in such a way that the needle stayed firmly in the groove when it was played but gave you plenty of thump; it was getting the correct equalization of frequency (eq) between the guitars, drums and bass. It was miking the drums well, too: before the Beatles many groups didn't put a microphone on the bass drum. They would put a mike about four feet away from the drums, pointing in the general direction of them, and hope for the best; ditto the bass guitar (there was no direct injection of the guitar into the recording console then, of course). Paul insisted that we get a really good bass sound, and I realized that we would have to make sure and mike his bass up much better, much closer than was normal practice then. So we taught each other what was required, the Beatles and I. We groped our way jointly towards an exciting sound.

We must have done something right, because later on, even much later on, recording artists would come up to me and say, in their turn, 'Why can't we get our records to sound like the Beatles tracks?' They would listen to the bass guitar on 'Baby You're A Rich Man' and say, 'Hey, man, that's a terrific bass sound. How the hell did you get a bass sound like that? Make ours sound that good!'

But, really, underneath it all was the driving power of the blues, demanding loudness.

Nothing's that simple, though . . .

Many influences other than the blues went into the Beatles' seemingly uncomplicated sound. Having gone on about the blues, I think the blues influence was much more important to John, George and Ringo than it was to Paul. If you look at McCartney songs like 'Yesterday', or 'Here, There, And Everywhere', there is little or no sign of a blues influence at all. There is more Elgar in them than there is John Lee Hooker.

Paul's father played in a local dance band from way back, remember, knocking out American popular, as opposed to pop music. They were melodies of the type I played as a lad with my own outfit, George Martin and his Four Tune Tellers. (I kid you not!) We performed songs from the films; Glenn Miller, Woody Herman , Jimmy Dorsey. If we were being adventurous, we would play a spot of boogie, old (aged) classics like Meade Lux Lewis's 'Honky Tonk Train Blues', or a Jimmy Yancey number. My band played about twice a week, mainly at dances, the dances in question being the fox-trot and the quickstep. You get the picture.

In those days only the rougher bands in Britain played jazz. (As for playing the blues, that was like being a musical Hell's Angel!) I am sure the dance hall standards were what Jim McCartney was playing too, and what the young Paul's ears drank in when they came up about level with his dad's piano keys.

Paul says his dad liked to play boogie-woogie on the piano, which is interesting when you look at Paul's own development into one of the world's great bass guitarists. In a boogie piano tune, the bass line, played by the left hand, produces a strong contrapuntal melody, rather than just a rhythmic thud. Paul's own bass guitar playing is of course the most melodic ever. He set a standard no one has ever reached. Sometimes he even composed songs around a bass line melody. Paul's bass line on 'Baby You're A Rich Man' is a good example of what he can do.

Then there was the completely unpredictable influence of George Harrison. From the mid-sixties onwards, George took Beatles music along a road that had nothing whatsoever to do with his own background or culture, or with American music for that matter: he took it east. The Cowboy Culture was not for him – George was an altogether cooler dude. Although initially hooked by the music of Elvis Presley, he soon gave a different cast entirely to the Beatles' output, composing tracks that were about a light year away from their other songs. He added a whole new range of Indian instruments to the Beatles' equation, instruments that crop up over and over on Beatles' tracks throughout their career, and make their sound unlike anything anyone else has done before or since. George Harrison is a dark horse all right, a one-off. He marches to the sound of a different drum.

As if all this were not quite enough to be going on with, there was my own part in the proceedings. I suppose I brought two major influences to bear on Beatles music: my formal training in classical music, and my love of experimental recording techniques.

One more thing, since we are on the subject of influences: the Beach Boys. The Beach Boys' style of singing and the song-writing style of Brian Wilson were major influences on the Beatles in the run-up to *Sgt. Pepper* – as they themselves freely acknowledged. (The reverse was also true.) Wilson's contrapuntal writing on *Pet Sounds* was something the Beatles didn't understand or think of in that rather alienating term, but it enthused them and fired up their own song writing. Their own harmonies started to get more complicated: the voices started to 'answer' one another. 'She's Leaving Home' is a two-part contrapuntal piece: the two human voices, John's and Paul's, interweave and complement one another (and are in turn pointed up by the strings). The Beach Boys, until *Pepper* at least, were more skilled at doing this kind of thing than John, Paul, George and Ringo. 'God Only Knows', track eight on the Beach Boys' *Pet Sounds* album, really made the Beatles sit up and take notice of the opposition. After all, the opposition had been listening closely to them:

> **In December of 1966 [sic – he must mean 1965], I heard the album *Rubber Soul* by the Beatles. It was definitely a challenge for me. I saw that every cut was very artistically interesting and stimulating. I immediately went to work on the songs for *Pet Sounds*.** — Brian Wilson's sleeve notes to *Pet Sounds*

I was really blown away with how clever it [*Pet Sounds*] was and how intriguing the arrangements were ... because of the work they'd done it didn't seem too much of a stretch for us to get further out than they'd got; so it was very influential.

— Paul, *South Bank Show*

Pet Sounds preceded *Pepper*. When he heard *Pepper*, Brian Wilson reportedly abandoned the album he was working on and retired hurt for a few months. He must have had a major rethink during that time, because the next Beach Boys album, *Good Vibrations*, was certainly another corker.

They were battles in a war, these albums: a curious transatlantic slugging match, a rivalry conducted by means of song writing and recording genius. The Beatles thought *Pet Sounds*, its vocal harmonies in particular, was a fantastic album. I thought it was great, too. 'Could we do as well as that?' they asked me, in the run-up to their own new long-player. 'No,' I replied. 'We can do better.'

We did.

A happy confusion of tides and cross-currents came together in the music of the Beatles, but in the end they are only a background murmur.

The single biggest factor in the brilliance of the Beatles' music was and always will remain – their own talent.

CHAPTER SIX

19 January 1967:
'Well I just had to laugh . . .'

Very few Beatles' tracks are more original, or more gripping when you first hear them, than the next track we recorded for the new album, 'A Day In The Life'.

John brought his initial ideas to Paul and they sat down in the music room upstairs at Cavendish Avenue to work together on the song. I must confess that I had always thought, like most people, that the lyric *'he blew his mind out in a car'* referred to the death of Tara Browne, who was a close friend of John and Paul. Not so. Some Beatle analyst somewhere had put two and two together to make five. In fact the marvellous lyrics that the composers concocted had nothing to do with a car crash. But it was a drug reference, as was *'I'd love to turn you on'*. They had been imagining a stoned politician who had stopped at some traffic lights.

John's inspiration for lyrics often came from things he had observed or read.

I was writing the song with the *Daily Mail* propped up in front of me on the piano. I had it open at their News in Brief, or Far and Near, whatever they call it. There was a paragraph about 4000 holes in Blackburn, Lancashire, being discovered and there was still one word missing in that verse when we came to record. I knew the line had to go, 'Now they know how many holes it takes to . . . the Albert Hall.' It was a nonsense verse really, but for some reason I couldn't think of the verb. What did the holes do to the Albert Hall? It was Terry Doran, a friend, who said, 'Fill the Albert Hall.'
— Hunter Davies, *The Beatles* (Heinemann)

Bob Dylan was a strong influence on John. He showed that you could write lyrics that had punch, pith, and bite; that reflected, say, intimate personal experience – or political anger.

Other influences on John, sworn to by those who were closest to him, are harder to detect. John's guardian Aunt Mimi, for instance, once said she 'saw a lot of Balzac in John's songs ...' Whatever can she have meant by that? She tells us, in Ray Coleman's biography of him, *John Winston Lennon*, that her ward had a voracious appetite for Honoré de Balzac's short stories, a large collection of which could be found on her bookshelves.

Well, Balzac's use of realism – historical, economic, social – is all-pervasive. Realism is a way of making his stories seem true-to-life, among the other things he uses it for. Here is John on the same subject:

Rock 'n' roll was real, everything else was unreal. And the thing about rock 'n' roll, good rock 'n' roll, whatever 'good' means, is that it's real, and realism gets through to you despite yourself. You recognise something in it which is true, like all true art.

– John Lennon Remembers

He certainly wrote about the thing that was most real to him, which was his own everyday life. And 'A Day In The Life' is a pretty good example of that.

In the early days John wrote some very effective, very simple songs based on the guitar, but his love of word-play, his sheer sense of fun with words, was always right to the fore when he was composing. From the very start of his musical career he was writing down the verbal fireworks displays that would later become his funny, witty books – and his songs.

I remember a trip to the seaside at Margate, where the Beatles were appearing in some variety theatre or other – it might even have been an appearance on the end of the pier – these were very early days! Judy and I had gone along to keep them company. John was scribbling down the beginnings of *In His Own Write* into a little notebook; silly words, nonsense words like Edward Lear's *Jabberwocky*, warm and readable and entertaining. Judy looked over at what he had written, liked it, and started reading it out loud.

51

Judy Lockhart Smith's upper-crust accent, reading John Lennon's words, made everybody fall around with laughter:

It were a small village, Squirmly on the Slug, and vile ruperts spread fat and thick amongst the inhabidads what libed there.

One victor of these gossipity tongues had oft been Victor Hardly, a harmless boot, whom never halmed nobody. A typical quimmty old hag who spread these vile ruperts was Mrs Weatherby – a widow by her first husbands.

'They're holding a Black Matt down at Victor's pad,' was oft heard about the village – but I never heard it. Things like this were getting Victor down, if not lower...

The Beatles were beside themselves, rolling about as these strange half-nonsensical words came tripping off Judy's silken tongue. It was then that we all realized how kooky, how entirely off-the-wall some of John's thoughts and lyrics really were; and that Jabberwockyness developed enormously as time went on. The lyrics were a more important part of John's songs than they were in some of Paul's. It would be silly to say that John ignored the music, but the lyrics generally drove the composition of his songs.

We did a first run-through of 'A Day In The Life' on 19 January, with Paul on piano, John singing and playing acoustic guitar, Ringo on bongo drums, and George on maracas. On that first take, John counts in on the tape by saying, 'Sugar plum fairy, sugar plum fairy ...' which does nothing to diminish the belief that he was taking drugs on *Pepper*! (A 'sugar plum fairy', in drugs parlance, is the person who brings you your dope, or whatever.) This first stab at recording 'A Day In The Life' concentrated on the bare bones of the song, which so far had no middle section.

Track 1: basic backing of the entire record: piano, guitar, maracas and bongo.

Track 4: John's vocal, already with heavy tape echo on it. John always hated his voice, always wanted something done to it. In this

BEATLES UNPLUGGED *As they were when I first met them, 1962*

WE'VE GOT A NEW DRUMMER *The first real session, 1962*

BRIAN WITH HIS 'BOYS'

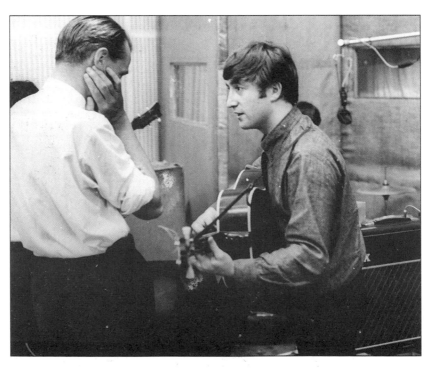

IT GOES LIKE THIS *John plays me a new song*

HEAD ARRANGEMENT *George, Paul, John and their producer, 1963*

BIGGER THAN JESUS? *John explains, 1966*

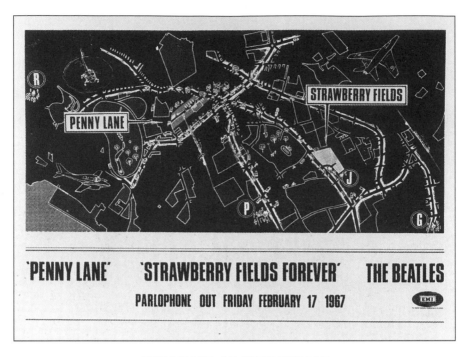

THE HEART OF LIVERPUDDLE
EMI's advertisement for the first single not to get to Number One on release

'WELL, THAT'S IT, I'M NOT A BEATLE ANY MORE'
The Beatles at the beginning of the Sgt. Pepper *recording, 1967*

A DAY IN THE LIFE *Improvisation at 1.37 a.m.*

**WITH VERY LITTLE HELP
FROM MY FRIENDS**

**WRITER AND PRODUCER
SEEING EYE TO EYE**

WITHIN ME, WITHOUT ME
George in pensive mood

**JOHN ALWAYS LIKED
A BIT OF BRASS**

INNER LIGHT
John, George, Ringo, Patti Boyd with the Maharishi in Bangor, August 1967

**THERE WILL BE A
SHOW TONIGHT...**
The original Benefit for Mr Kite

THE FAB FOUR WITH THE FAB FOUR
The press launch of Pepper *at Brian
Epstein's house*

ON THE SOFA *CHEZ* EPSTEIN

THE GREAT MINDS BEHIND THE ALBUM SLEEVE

case he said he wanted to 'sound like Elvis Presley on "Heartbreak Hotel"'. So we put the image of the voice about 90 milliseconds behind the actual voice itself. As the voice goes past the record head it obviously records. The playback head is situated after the record head, so you hear the voice later. In the old days, we used to do tape echo that way: take the voice off the playback head and feed as much as you wanted of it back into the record head. (Nowadays you do it by means of digital delay.) Geoff Emerick says that to get that echo, he fed John's vocal on to a mono tape machine, then took the output of that, because the record/replay heads on a mono machine were separate, then fed it back on itself over and over again until he got a twittery kind of vocal sound.

John was listening to this in his cans, and hearing so much distortion on his voice made him feel really happy. John's liking for stupendous amounts of echo stemmed from his early teens. When he was very young and learning to play the guitar, a maddened Aunt Mimi would frequently banish him to the porch of their Menlove Avenue semi. The porch's acoustics gave his voice a natural echo, and he grew up used to it sounding like that. It seemed normal to him. John also discovered early on in his career that tape echo came in handy for his sense of rhythm: when the delay on the tape was right it helped him to keep time.

In fact, John's voice on this first run-through was marvellous, as usual.

We still had to include a middle eight on the song, so we recorded our roadie Mal Evans on this track, Track 4, as well. His job was to count down the twenty-four bars in the middle of 'A Day In The Life' that were still blank. Why twenty-four bars? Why not?

John asked Paul if he could think of anything for this yawning space. Paul had written a scrap of song, which John liked: 'Woke up, fell out of bed, Dragged a comb across my head . . .' So they agreed to put that in. But it was Paul's idea to have something really tumultuous on the song, something that would whack the person listening right between the ears and leave them gasping with shock. He didn't know quite what it was he wanted, but he did want to try for something extremely startling.

Paul was carrying the backing to the song on the piano. During that twenty-four-bar gap, all you could hear was his piano banging away, with a lot of wrong notes, some of them deliberate, the dissonance increasing as his playing got more frenzied towards the end. To keep everyone together, and so that we would know when we were due back into the song proper again, Mal Evans counted the bars out loud. This sounded very dull – 'One, two, three . . . ' – so we put an increasing amount of tape echo on his voice, too: at the end there was a tremendous amount of reverb on it.

Just to make sure that everyone knew when to restart, we added an alarm clock at the end of the final bar. This was really not trying to be clever, not at this stage, anyway. We were a bit bored and the clock was just a little joke. As it happened, the alarm going off fitted perfectly with the lyrics that started Paul's middle section to the song, 'Woke up, got out of bed . . . ' so the bell stayed in.

Before we went home, John overdubbed a couple of extra vocal takes, on Tracks 2 and 3 (we had his original vocals on Track 4). In the end, I selected Track 2 as the best, but while John was recording on Track 3, Paul added some heavy piano chords at the beginning of the song, a few bars in, at the end of the instrumental introduction.

We came back to the song the following day, a Friday. I mixed everything down on to two new tracks of a second tape: all the piano, guitar, maracas, bongo drums on Track 1, and a mix of John's various vocals, complete with echo, on Track 2. In some cases we double-tracked John's voice, overlaying what we'd recorded the previous day. Next, Paul overdubbed his bit, laying down his vocal for the new middle section of the song, the 'Woke up, got out of bed . . . ' segment. Rather than use up any further tracks on this new, mixed-down tape, I dropped Paul's vocals on to it, in between John's own. All the vocals were now on one track.

Once he had listened to them, Paul thought he could make a better job of his vocals, and he had another stab at them on 3 February. Track 3 we used up recording Ringo's wonderful drum-track combination of bass drum, cymbals and famous tom-tom sound, which he re-recorded that evening, and Paul laid down his bass guitar track at the same time. Ringo and Paul recorded simultaneously, because I didn't want to waste any more precious tracks.

We had been keeping Track 4 of this second tape free for orchestral work, but Paul used it to lay down still more piano.

On analogue tape, every time you transfer one track to another, you multiply the signal-to-noise ratio. Dirt comes up, all the background hiss and audio clutter, and this noise multiplies by the square of each tape-to-tape transfer. Two copies create four times the amount of noise; a third generation increases the noise by nine times! So I had to be very disciplined in keeping the track usage together.

Producers today would be horrified at such restrictions – they are used to recording every sound on its own track. Because of this good-housekeeping requirement, Paul would be aware that if he made a mistake with his bass playing, he might be ruining a great take from Ringo; and Ringo would be thinking the same thing about his own performance. It was an added spur for them to play well . . .

I joined the band because they were the best musicians around in Liverpool, and I wanted to be with that . . . – Ringo, *South Bank Show*

By the time we finished the session on 20 January (in fact it was about 1 a.m. on the 21st), I loved the song: John's dry, deadpan voice, Paul's bouncy middle segment acting as a foil to that, and I really liked the chords that got us back to John's section, which was in a different key. We were not sure then what else we wanted to do to it, so we left it for a bit, to think. We often worked in this way, starting something new to give us more time on another song in progress. It was the painter laying aside the canvas, starting a new work, then coming back to the first work afresh, able to see at once what was good or bad about it, and what needed to be done by way of improvement.

In the meantime, Paul came up with idea of the *Sgt. Pepper* title song, which we began recording.

I needed a break from recording 'A Day In The Life', in any case, because I had to do some scoring for orchestra. The Beatles had come to me and said they wanted a symphony orchestra. Paul fancied the idea more than the others. 'Nonsense,' I replied. 'You cannot, cannot have a symphony orchestra just for a few chords, Paul. Waste of money. I mean you're talking about ninety musicians! This is EMI, not Rockefeller!' Thus spake the well-trained corporate lackey still lurking somewhere inside me. Yet my imagination was fired: a symphony orchestra! I could see at once that we could make a lovely sound.

I thought very hard. The song did need a grand flourish of some sort. This crazy idea might just work. We had never used a symphony orchestra before; we'd used a string quartet, an octet, the odd trumpet or a sax section, so the notion of a great leap forward into a full-sized orchestra was very appealing – and kind of logical. It is one of the biggest toys you can play with. But ninety musicians would be expensive; too expensive.

'What do you want this symphony orchestra to do, exactly?' I asked, stalling for time. I really was not sure that it had been properly thought out. But Paul had been listening to a lot of avant-garde music by the likes of John Cage, Stockhausen, and Luciano Berio. He had told John he would like to include an instrumental passage with this avant-garde feel. He had the idea to create a spiralling ascent of sound, suggesting we start the passage with all instruments on their lowest note and climbing to the highest in their own time.

I decided half a symphony orchestra would do – smaller string section, single woodwind and brass – and settled on forty one musicians. Cheeseparer! Honour was satisfied, but I knew it was of little use telling them to improvise. They were used to working from written parts, no matter how strange. I suppose it was difficult for the Beatles to fully understand that. They had never needed a note of written music in their lives. Why should anyone else? Of course, if we had approached the symphony musicians in those days without a prepared score they would have laughed us out of court.

When I sat down to write the score, I realized that John had not come up with anything for the first few notes the orchestra would have to play, after he stops singing, 'I'd love to turn you on . . . ' He sings this line in a very characteristic manner, the tune wavering between semitones. This, I thought, would be a great phrase to echo, so I wrote a very slow semitone trill for the strings, bowing with a gentle *portamento* and increasing gradually in frequency and intensity. This gives a suitably mysterious effect, making a good introduction or bridge to the now famous dissonant orchestral climb that is unique to this song.

The twenty-four-bar gap we were now going to fill needed notes, even though the 'slope up' – the climb – did not. What we did over those twenty-four bars was to instruct each musician to begin by playing the lowest note on their instrument (as quietly as they could!), and to finish at the end of the final bar by playing their loudest and highest note. The main thing I had to accomplish with this score was to give the orchestra signposts: the twenty-four vacant bars took quite a long time to get through – about forty seconds – and the musicians were supposed to be gradually sliding up, very, very slowly, and as smoothly as possible. The strings weren't playing notes, just slithering away.

The woodwind and some of the brass instruments had to play distinct notes, although some players could lip, rather than tongue, their notes to make a smoother transition from one note to the next. At each bar line I marked in an approximation of where each musician should be, like so many way points along a musical route.

When it came to the recording, I was counting out the bars as they went through them, so they knew that when they got to bar six, for example, they should be at A flat, or whatever. Having given them the score, I had to tell them how to play it. The instructions given, though, shook them rigid. Here was a top flight orchestra, who had been taught all their lives by maestros that they must play as one coherent unit. I told them that the essential thing in this case was *not* to play like the fellow next to them! 'If you do listen to the guy next to you,' I told them, 'and you find you're playing the same note, you're playing the wrong note. I want you to go your own way, and just ignore everything else; just make your own sound.' They laughed; half of them thought we were completely insane, and the others thought this was a great hoot.

As the Beatles had never had a symphony orchestra before, they wanted to make the recording a special occasion. 'Will you wear evening dress,' they asked me, 'and will you get the orchestra to wear evening dress?'

'Are *you* going to?' I asked.

'Yeah,' they came back. 'We'll do it!'

'All right,' I said. 'If you wear evening dress, I'll wear evening dress.' They didn't, of course, but they wore their version of it: outrageously flamboyant floral costumes. Not quite *Sgt. Pepper* costumes, but very flower power. For some reason known only to himself, Paul, for example, arrived wearing a full-length red cook's apron, which clashed horribly with his purple-and-black sub-Paisley pattern shirt!

They were determined to have a party, so they invited along a few of their mates – only about forty or so, including Mick Jagger, Marianne Faithfull, Pattie Harrison, Brian Jones, Simon Posthuma and Marijke Koger of the design team the Fool, Graham Nash, all of them wearing long, multicoloured flowing robes, stripy 'loon' flared pants, brilliant waistcoats, gaudy silk neckerchiefs, love-beads, bangles, baubles, badges and bells. Mingling discreetly in amongst all this unisex hippy flamboyance was Judy, wearing, of all things, a tweed suit – very fashionable!

People were running around with sparklers and blowing bubbles through little clay pipes. There was a funny rich smell in the air, which may of course just have been the joss-sticks that were burning all over the place . . .

It was a happening. As soon as the recording got under way, I told the flower-children to sit around the walls and behave them-selves; and, just like good children, they did!

After I'd run the orchestra through to make sure they had got their notes right (or should that be wrong?), I went back to Geoff in the control room to make sure he was getting it all down on tape. Also, I had a technical worry: I'd already filled up my tracks and wanted to be sure that the rough synchronization Ken Townsend had been fixing up for us was ready.

I was in the control-room with Ken and Geoff for about ten minutes. When I came back into the studio the party was in full swing. The Beatles had been among the evening-dressed orchestra handing out carnival novelties. Erich Gruenberg, leader of the second violins, was playing with a monkey's paw on his bowing hand and wearing coloured paper spectacles. David McCallum, the leader of the London Philharmonic (and father of *The Man From U.N.C.L.E.* actor), was wearing a very large red nose. There was a balloon on the end of the bassoon, which went up and down as the bassoonist played. I stared at it all and started laughing. It was a riot. 'Come on,' said Paul, 'join in, George. Let's have some fun.' 'But Paul,' I replied. 'You said fun is the one thing that money can't buy!'

Of course, in its way it was fun. But at the back of my mind – all the time – was the thought that this was a very expensive way of letting our hair down. I had an urge to get this thing structured, a fear that it might break down into complete chaos and the whole effort go to waste. I was pretty nervous, in short.

During the course of my career I had either worked with the forty-one musicians we used that evening, (they were all men – women had not then been liberated in the world of British classical music), or I had met them some other way. Erich Gruenberg, for example, had won the Max Rostal prize when we were both at the Guildhall School of Music. Knowing them all so well definitely helped calm my nerves on this particular occasion!

All the time, Geoff was tweaking away at the studio's in-built 'ambiophony' system, which instantly fed the music back through the hundred speakers spaced around the studio walls to create a customized – and highly amplified – sound.

We recorded 'A Day In The Life' on three different tapes; very unusual for the Beatles. Tape 1 had the rhythm backing and John's voice. We dubbed those down on the second day, adding extra vocals, together with the first track of the orchestral recording. Then we added four more tracks of the orchestral recording, making five in all. The orchestra actually performed five separate times, and each time they were distinctly different. On the last take of all, for example, there is lots more timpani – drums – than on the previous attempts.

When we were satisfied with the orchestral material, we had to synchronize it with our original four-track master. This was difficult, to say the least. Nowadays it is dead easy to lock tapes together in perfect synchronicity: an electronic code called SMPTE, currently indispensable in recording studios, does the job. In 1967, though, nothing like that existed. There was the hit-or-miss method of jump-starting the tape machines together by hand. But this was extremely difficult to pull off, and usually meant the speeds of the two machines would differ by a tiny but noticeable amount. And sooner or later they would drift out of time. This was where Ken Townsend and his ingenuity came in. Realizing I would be in trouble, he had been cooking up a scheme to run the machines in synch. And it almost worked!

Ken's idea was to run an identical 50-hertz pulse to the capstans of each tape machine so that one would kick-start the other, in exactly the same way, every time, on time. Even with that achieved, the process of hitting the same exact musical start-point on two separate machines was still a matter of trial and error. It required a great deal of patience and understanding. I kept the Beatles well away from the scene of the action while all this was going on!

Looking back on those ancient times, I still wonder at the primitive state of our art. If I were to do it again, I would have no qualms about booking the entire London Symphony Orchestra several times over. But I am not convinced it would be any more effective: our string and sealing-wax methods did the job all right. If you listen closely to the original recording, though, you can hear the orchestra going in and out of time. It's not their bad playing – just our crude synchronization system falling down on the job.

'A Day In The Life' was something special, even before it had the orchestral orgasm grafted on to it. It was and is a great song. John's vocal on it really did something for me. I was always enormously captivated by his voice, and on this track it is at its best. I miss hearing that voice terribly.

Having done all the orchestral bit, we wanted something to finish off the song. When you reached that high note at the close of the orchestral sequence you were left hanging there; the song needed bringing sharply back down to earth. What we required, I thought, was a simple yet stunning chord. Something very, very loud, very resonant. But what would give us that resonance? I decided to try out a notion which went back to the recording of 'Tomorrow Never Knows': the '4000 monks' ploy. I had always thought that the sound of a lot of people chanting a mantra was impelling and hypnotic. 'Why don't we make a chord of people singing, to make a noise like a gigantic tamboura?' I suggested. 'Get them to sing all the basic notes, with maybe a few fifths in between, and track them, over and over and over again, to give it depth?'

So we did that, and there is a tape of it at Abbey Road in the vaults. If I had had 4000 people available to sing, it might have worked. As it is, the noise that came out the other end is absolutely pathetic! I had eight or nine people, multiplied four or five times. Nobody had enough breath to hold the chord beyond about fifteen or twenty seconds, so it petered out, anyway, long before it should have done.

So we moved smartly on to a second idea: a gigantic piano chord. You get a wonderful sound from a piano if you let the overtones work. Try it for yourself: if you have a piano in your house, open the lid wide, press down the sustain pedal (the right one), lean over, and shout. You will hear the piano singing back to you all the little notes that are in your voice. When there are many of those overtones working against each other, they generate extra frequencies, so-called 'beat' frequencies, which give a wonderful kind of rolling effect. Now multiply that a thousand times . . .

We managed to scrape together three pianos. After a few hilarious practice shots, Paul, John, Ringo, Mal Evans and I crunched down on the same chord as hard as we could. You can hear my voice on the master tape counting in to the chord, so that everyone hits it at exactly the same time.

If you recorded a heavy chord strike like that on a piano without any compression, you would hear a very, very loud note to begin with, but the die-away would be very quiet. We wanted the first impact of the chord to be there (although not overbearing), but the decay to be very loud. (Compression takes the impact of the note, absorbs it like a shock absorber, then brings the volume back up quickly to compensate.) As the chord started to fade, Geoff Emerick raised the gain gradually, to keep it singing on. At the end of the note, forty-five seconds into it, the volume level on the studio amplifiers was enormous.

Everybody had to be terribly quiet. If anybody were to have coughed, it would have sounded like an explosion. As it is, on the special Ultra High Quality Recording edition of *Sgt. Pepper*, you can hear the Abbey Road air-conditioning system purring away in the background as Geoff opens the volume faders to the stops at the very end of the die-away. That's how we got the famous piano chord.

If a string broke on John's guitar, he would be looking around for someone to repair it. His favourite line was, 'I'm sure you can fix it . . .' whether he was talking about a song or a piece of equipment. Sometimes, if he were forced to fix whatever was wrong with a song without any help, the results could be brilliant. If he had to mend a fuse, he was liable to electrocute himself. If he had to fix a song, however, he could apply a lateral, unpredictable spin to it that had genius all over it.

John and I had a good understanding; I could get pretty close to what he wanted. But this very understanding sometimes became a bit of a problem. As far as John was concerned, if the recording process was a well-oiled mechanism, it was routine – and therefore Establishment. The rebel in John was always looking to kick over the traces. He was still a dear man, even though he could be very difficult to please at times.

Looking back at our collaborations, I think that John was suspicious if my role looked too easy. He had a genuine awe for technical matters outside his experience, oddly mixed up with a blithe expectation of immediate and unfailing technical excellence. Although he was the least technical Beatle, he did not have much regard for the brilliant work done by the Abbey Road staff, and could never understand why we were limited in our number of recording tracks. I could understand his frustration, as I too believed we should be supplied with the very latest and best equipment. I could see, though, that EMI in its Abbey Road manifestation was not unlike Rolls-Royce at the time: a little conservative, but still staffed by cracking engineers.

It was this childlike scepticism that made John easy prey for those who promised him instant wizardry. Though I was no longer part of the Abbey Road staff, I was irritated on their behalf when John told me that his new-found friend 'Magic' Alex Mardas was on the point of perfecting a recording system with no fewer than seventy-two tracks. Of course, it all turned out to be rubbish, but John would believe every word, especially when presented with a little matchbox-sized toy that made electronic sounds – slung together in a jiffy by the Greek wizard.

CHAPTER SEVEN

1 February 1967: 'We hope you will enjoy the show . . .'

. . . it was all very Uncle Joe's Medicine Show, with dancing birds and the elixir of life . . .

– Paul, *South Bank Show*

'Sgt. Pepper's Lonely Hearts Club Band' was the song that triggered the whole idea of the album becoming a 'concept' album. In a bizarre way, it may have been the king himself, Elvis Presley, who inspired the idea. Apparently he once sent his Cadillac on tour without accompanying it. This crazy ploy was something the Beatles marvelled at and often joked about, so an idea was spawned which grew in all their minds: 'Why don't we make an album that is a show, and send *that* on tour instead of ourselves?' This was a radical, even fanciful idea at that time, but the Beatles could immediately see the possibilities and potential in it. It might just be a way round the problem of their not touring any more. Was it a commercially viable idea, though? Television did not yet have the vice-like grip on the business of pop that it has now. Live performances were the only real means by which a band could satisfy public demand. Could an album, however good, be an effective substitute for a live tour? Would the fans wear it?

Whatever the answer, the Beatles were determined to give the new album something that they'd never had before – time.

Wherever Paul dreamt it up, and he says it came to him while he was on a plane, the idea of writing a song about a fictitious band called Sgt Pepper's Lonely Hearts Club Band gradually grew into the Beatles actually being that band. If there was any concept, that was it – the *doppelgänger* Beatles. As to Sgt. Pepper, who was he and where did he come from?

63

Mal Evans, Beatles roadie, gets the credit in some quarters for thinking up the actual name. He came up with 'Salt and Pepper' which developed into one of Paul's *alter egos*. As for the rest of it, the idea of the travelling show and all, that comes from the same place as Eleanor Rigby and Father MacKenzie, or Lovely Rita: from the fertile fields of Paul's imagination.

Some of the details of the album's very first origins are becoming lost in the mists of time and our unreliable memories. For example, it is said that the original idea was to do an album about the boys' Liverpool childhood, a real nostalgia trip. This at least explains 'Strawberry Fields Forever', 'Penny Lane' and 'When I'm Sixty-Four'. As part of this thematic journey down memory lane, so the story goes, the band was to be a fictitious North of England brass band – hence the brass instruments the boys are clutching on the album cover. (Other people will tell you that the band was meant to be a German marching band.) I had a word with Neil Aspinall about this and he thinks it is all tosh. So do I.

Whatever the truth of the matter, Paul liked brass bands, and he wanted one in. (He later indulged his liking for the sound by using a genuine brass band on the sound-track of the Boulting Brothers film *The Family Way*: music by Paul, score by me. He also recorded one of Britain's most famous brass outfits, the Black Dyke Mills Band, for Apple Records.)

... it was going to be a whole show, but after two tracks everybody started getting fed up and doing their own songs again ... – Ringo, *South Bank Show*

There was one thing that the Beatles were absolutely determined about. Every single element of this album must add value to the project as a whole: from the songs, the album cover, the technical production, everything was to play its role in making something entirely different – and entirely good. This was the new baby: they wanted the best for it. Hence the revolutionary gatefold sleeve, with the lyrics printed on it for the first time, the extraordinary expense and effort that went into the cover photograph, the unprecedented amount of time and care that went into the technical production.

You put the record on, and you hear the audience; you hear the band warming up, and the show opens with their theme tune. This in turn merges into the first star solo, with the Billy Shears character singing his song. After he has finished, that show, that world we have entered disappears, and we are taken into a completely different world, a world of tangerine trees and marmalade skies. So it goes on through the album. It is only at the end that the original show theme comes back, when you hear the band tuning up again, the murmurs of the concert hall. This reprise just about manages to convince us that we have been listening to a rounded and coherent performance, when we have in fact been listening to a series of little side-shows, each with its own distinct personality.

The title song is really a good old-fashioned rocker, but it pulls people into the album with its illusion of a live performance. By adding the sound effects of applause, tuning up, and so on, we tried to paint a tableau: of the curtain going up and seeing the band on the stage. Once again, we were trying to create the illusion of being able to shut one's eyes and see a complete picture, created by music. Sgt. Pepper's band really was up there blasting away for us. In fact, of all the songs on the album, the opening song was the nearest we got to a fully fledged live performance in the studio. It was a 'live' show in its own right, every time, even though only a privileged few of us ever saw it.

We had been thinking from the start of linking up the title song with Ringo's 'A Little Help From My Friends'. But it was only when we were a long way down the road, at the stage of recording the four French horns, that the idea of recording the opening number as if it were a live performance came up.

We had to go to extreme lengths to convince people, using numerous sound-effects, that they were actually listening to a live show. It meant overdubbing that wonderful 'hush' of an audience before the performance starts, adding applause and laughter, and so on. So I used a recording I had made at a performance of 'Beyond the Fringe', a comedy revue I'd seen at London's Fortune Theatre in 1961, starring Peter Cook, Dudley Moore, Alan Bennett and Jonathan Miller. A lot of the atmosphere was wild-tracked from that show, but the tuning up sounds themselves came from the 'A Day In The Life' orchestra recording, on 10 February.

We started recording the title song on 1 February. Ironically for what was Britain's first 'concept' album, it was two months or so after we had first started work on the album. We did nine takes of the rhythm track that night, including the rehearsals. When we listened back we reckoned number nine was the best we had completed:

TRACK 1: rhythm – George and Paul on guitars, drums with heavy echo

TRACK 2: bass guitar

TRACK 3: vocal

TRACK 4: vocal (this one marked best)

The following day we came in and worked on Paul's main vocal, and the group's backing vocals, on Tracks 3 and 4. Paul sings his heart out on this one. Anyone who thinks that Paul McCartney is not a great singer of rock 'n' roll only has to listen to his voice on this track. You can hear the gravel in it.

With all our tracks now full, we had to go to another four-track tape. This time we put all the instruments on Track 1, and the vocals, with echo, we laid down on Track 4. We did a demo re-mix, and ran off some acetates so we could all listen to what we had done so far. Then we left the song, for what turned out to be a whole month.

When we came back in on the evening of 3 March the tape operator was Richard Lush. For some reason, John took him to one side and asked him to record all the conversations between the musicians. It was the beginning of John's obsession with recording. Later on, when he was with Yoko Ono, it seemed that John videotaped and recorded almost everything that happened in his life, from his first swallow of coffee in the morning until his eyelids closed at night.

Somewhere in Yoko's vast archives is me talking to a French horn player about that session. It must be very edifying . . .!

All we did that evening was to put French horns on to Track 3, then drop George Harrison's guitar solo into the gaps remaining on that track. It was a pretty good solo, too: even if it took seven hours to record.

Now, on this new, second tape, we were just about through. We had vocals and echo on Track 4, horns and lead guitar on Track 3, and all the rhythm sounds on Track 1. The special effects, audience noise, etc., we added on 6 March, on to Track 2, and on this day we finished the mixing. A good, speedy job all round, that one.

Apart from sorting out the four horns, I did not have much to do with the musical arrangement of the Sgt. Pepper track. The boys took to the simple tune like the proverbial ducks to water and made up the arrangement as they went along. You could tell how much they enjoyed playing a straightforward rocker, because it fairly hummed along.

The song got its enormous momentum from the driving guitars and drums: Paul and George play a double quaver beat on guitars on the first and third beats of the bar of the chorus, leaving space for Ringo's heavy snare on the second and fourth beats. Paul insisted on doing the guitar solos himself, in the end, which may well have irritated George.

Before concept albums became a dirty word, you'd put it on and sit down and say, 'Oh well, for the next fifty minutes I'm going to be going there. So it was very new from that point of view.

– Phil Collins, *South Bank Show*

Having started out with only the vaguest idea of what they wanted to do with their new album, the Beatles were now beginning to do something very exciting indeed with it. The essence is freedom.

Most sizeable record companies stare fixedly at one thing and one thing only: the bottom line. Profits are the be all and end all. They see the work of a recording artist as a product, to be sold, like any other. This can and does lead inevitably to conflicts of interest; in fact it sometimes leads to bloody and protracted warfare between an artist and a record company.

Consequently record companies tend to be very conservative in their view of what a successful recording artist should be doing. If they get a hit, they want another one: they do not, generally speaking, want anything different. The major Hollywood studios view the film market in the same way: if *Star Trek* turns out to be a winning formula, don't go and make *Howard's End*, they tell you, give us *Star Trek II*, and *III*, and *IV*, and *Star Trek XVII*, if necessary . . . Cash in! The problem is, it gets very boring, and it is completely unimaginative.

So a recording artist is expected by his or her owners to keep doing more or less the same thing, provided it continues to sell. But most artists don't want to do that; they want to learn, and evolve. My own view is and always has been that artists should be able to grow, to blossom. They should not have to stand still for reasons of simple profit.

When the Beatles announced that they were going into the studio for an indefinite period, before *Pepper*, I had some interesting and fairly taut discussions with the powers that be at EMI, who were understandably nervous about what would come of it all. Luckily for me, the Beatles never let me down. Whenever I said, 'Give them their heads, let them do different things,' they came up with things that were as good as, if not better than, the material they had been doing before. And it always sold.

One of my main jobs with the Beatles, as I saw it by 1967, was to give them as much freedom as possible in the studio, but to make sure that they did not come off the rails in the process.

The years between the age of nineteen and twenty-three are pretty important in anyone's life: but in those four years the Beatles had gone from relative obscurity to being, as Brian Epstein had always predicted, 'more famous than Elvis Presley'. They had shared this skyrocket trip to fame together, and had become, as a consequence, an impregnable quartet. No one else had gone through what they had, no one else understood. They seemed to find a tremendous inspiration from each other's presence. There was a kind of love between the four of them, some feeling that gave them strength. It was a case of the whole being stronger than the sum of its parts. Although the world had accepted then with open arms, it could also, in many ways, be their enemy. They were a bit like the four corners of a Guards Regiment 'square' on the battlefield at Waterloo – steadfast together against the media shot and shell.

While *Pepper* was being made they were helping each other, in their daily lives, more than at any other time.

They were easy to work with in the studio. They loved the whole process of recording: the studio was a playground, as far as they were concerned. We worked very long hours, often in the early hours of the morning, right from the word go. But by 1966 they were becoming even more demanding. They would ring up and say, 'We want to come in tonight at eight o'clock,' and everybody just had to be there – whatever else they might have on. I had reconciled myself to the fact that they would be my number one priority. The long hours were more a problem for me with regard to other recording artists than they were in terms of a personal life. Judy accepted it; so did I. But quite often Neil Aspinall would ring up in his role as Beatles' road manager and say, 'Look, George, we've got to have the studio at seven tonight,' and I would have to try to rearrange a session booked with somebody else who was quite important – but not as important as the Fab Four. Then the Beatles would turn up at ten! When it came right down to it, we were all their minions.

In the studio I was very much part of them; every voice was heard equally. But once they left the studio, out into the night, they closed themselves off again, reverting to their hermetically sealed unit. Even Brian Epstein didn't get inside that shell. As for the way they viewed me, I was 'very twelve-inch', in Ringo's memorable phrase. (Back in the fifties we used to issue ten-inch and twelve-inch vinyl records. The ten-inch records were the 'rhythm-style series', what we now call pop, and the twelve-inch were the cantatas and symphonies: the classical. Ten-inch was common; but twelve-inch – that was a cut above!)

In a BBC broadcast not long before he died, John spoke of our work together. He was obviously thinking about our times from *Revolver*, on through *Pepper* and beyond, when he said of me: 'He had a very great musical knowledge and background, so he could translate for us and suggest a lot of amazing technical things . . . We'd be saying we want it to go "Ooh-ooh!" and "Ee-ee!" and he'd say, "Oh, great! Great! Let's put it in here!" It's hard to say who did what . . . He taught us a lot and I'm sure we taught him a lot by our primitive musical ability.'*

I certainly did learn a lot from them, and their musical knowledge very rapidly became anything but primitive.

Tony King, who worked for us and was a good friend of John, remembers that our sessions were like 'all the fun of the fair. Everybody would have these funny sort of sixties smiles on their faces; and among all this madness was the Duke of Edinburgh, as we used to call George Martin.'*

*Both quotes from *In My Life – John Lennon Remembered*, by Kevin Howlett & Mark Lewisohn. BBC Publications.

John Lennon and Paul McCartney in particular were extremely good friends; they loved one another, really. They shared a spirit of adventure, and a modest little childhood ambition: they were going to go out and conquer the world. You could, though, almost touch the rivalry between them, it was so intense and so real, despite this overriding warmth. No sooner would John come up with an outstanding song evoking, say, his own early childhood, like 'Strawberry Fields Forever', than Paul answered him straight back with a winner in the same vein: 'Penny Lane'. It was typical of the way they worked as a song-writing duo. Creative rivalry kept them climbing their individual ladders – and kept the Beatles on top. John would write 'In My Life', and go up a rung; Paul would go one rung higher still with 'Yesterday'. Often they would help each other out on a song, if they were stuck – despite their dual composer credits. For the most part, though, they egged each other on by the brilliant example of their individual efforts.

We were very tight, the four of us, and very seldom did we let anybody in. But George won us over with his sense of humour; he actually did a Goons record, which means he's got to be OK ...

– Ringo, *South Bank Show*

8 February 1967: 'It's time for tea and meet the wife ...'

'Good Morning, Good Morning' was a John song, inspired by a television commercial for Kellogg's Corn Flakes. The advertisement had the line 'Good morning begins with Kellogg's' in it, which could be why there is a cock-crow on the song at the end – a tongue-in-cheek homage to the Kellogg's trademark.

John would often sit in his house trying to write a song at the piano, with the television on softly in the background at the same time. He tended to take more notice of the goggle-box when the composing was not going so well. Up came this commercial, and up popped the song!

At the time he was living in Weybridge, one of the poshest parts of the London commuter belt, in a twenty-seven-room 'stockbroker tudor' mansion. Much like Ringo, who was also married and lived just down the road (baby Zak had just arrived), John was leading a very suburban life. It was almost your pipe and slippers sort of thing – 'Did you have a good day at the office, dear?' routine.

Paul, on the other hand was unmarried, a bohemian sophisticated man-about-town, mixing with the artistic avant-garde, going to the 'right' galleries and theatre, reading the right underground magazines, leading an existence John and Ringo rather envied in some ways. George, meanwhile, had just married the glamorous Pattie Boyd.

Often enough, when John wanted to escape suburbia, he would drive up and spend the night at Paul's place in central London, not far from Abbey Road. John had to provide some sort of stable home-life for his wife and child, but he felt that the atmosphere at Weybridge was not conducive to good song writing.

I felt Paul was mixing with an unconventional crowd, but he was very conventional. Whereas John was being unconventional at home.

– Ringo, *South Bank Show* (unused transcript)

Judy and I went down to have dinner with John and Cynthia round about this time. Cyn had been an art student like John when they met in Liverpool, but marrying a Beatle had transformed her life. In the early days, Brian Epstein thought that news of a pregnant wife would drive away John's army of fans, so he insisted that she stay out of sight. Later, once the news had become public, Cynthia was allowed to join the Beatles on their travels; in fact she was with John on the very first US tour.

Intelligent and artistic, Cynthia found life in the Weybridge ghetto comfortable but distinctly limiting. She abandoned her art, either because of John or her son, or simply because she lost interest. Now, she had to have a regular life, not least for the sake of her Julian, who like any other child was going to school every day. It had been a pretty crazed existence before they settled down.

Anyway, when we arrived in Weybridge that evening, Cyn said that she had hoped to give us smoked salmon. She had sent out for it specially, to a local delicatessen, but time wore on, there was no sign of the order, and we all got hungrier and hungrier. The Lennons employed a married couple, who lived in a separate flat at the top, to look after the house. Judy dropped a little hint that perhaps Cyn's smoked salmon had been diverted to a different destination . . . A quick spot-check revealed the truth. Sure enough, them upstairs were having a great time eating our meal! So we made do with fish-paste sandwiches. We all had a laugh about it, but this little incident said something about their whole existence then.

It was frustrating for John seeing Paul swanning around, while he himself felt increasingly like a middle-class, middle-aged man. He had an extremely low boredom threshold, at the best of times.

Weybridge was bought for John. He had no idea, really, what he was letting himself in for when he agreed to let Brian Epstein find him a house there. It was a ghetto for rich people, and it still is: very safe, extremely well policed, and extremely secure. Many stars lived there – Tom Jones, Cliff Richard (who still does). It was a place to be, Weybridge, if you were big in the British media; much as Beverly Hills is to Hollywood now. It could have a pretty stultifying effect, if you let it. John was never surly about it all, though; when you went round to see him, he seemed happy. But part of him was looking for something more exciting.

In one way, Weybridge explains Yoko Ono's attractiveness to John: she was an antidote to the suburban mentality, if ever you met one.

She gave him the freedom to do all of that stuff that he really wanted to do. He couldn't really do it from the golf club. – Paul, on John's relationship with Yoko Ono

'Good Morning', then, is an ironic, not to say sarcastic look at that suburban life-style. Its lyrics make sharp little digs at the whole suburban deal: 'Everybody knows there's nothing doing, Everything is closed it's like a ruin, Everyone you see is half asleep . . . I've got nothing to say but it's OK, Good Morning . . . ' That just about summed up how he felt about his way of life at the time. (The line 'It's time for tea and meet the wife,' was culled from a rather banal British TV soap opera of the period, called, appropriately, *Meet the Wife*.)

'Good Morning, Good Morning' has a strange form. It starts off conventionally enough with an eight-bar introduction from the horns, followed by a raucous chant of the title from the boys. But the first verse has only ten beats in it. As John never once put pen to manuscript, it is anyone's guess where the bar lines lie. If you do happen to see a copy of the sheet music to this song, remember John had nothing to do with it; it was transcribed from the record by some chap in the Northern Songs publishing office.

In a ten-beat phrase there has to be an uneven bar somewhere, or else two bars of 5/4 – rare enough in pop music today and unheard of in 1967. The tempo is made even more complicated when the horns begin a new phrase under the last beat of the second verse. This is followed by the chant again: then, when we come back to the verse the horns play block chords to back the voice, stabbing accents in unusual spots, just to round off the complexity.

The basic tune was quite simple, but John wanted a very hard driving sound to punch it along. This is where the horns came in. I thought the way to do it would be to have a mixture of saxophones, trumpets and trombones playing either in unison or in octaves, and sometimes on spread chords. It so happened that Brian Epstein managed a group called Sounds Incorporated, who were good pals, if a bit crazy, so we brought them in to give us our horn sound. They worked with us all day on it – and they had a very hard time.

John's rhythms, so natural to his ear, were the very devil for the six players to deliver in perfect time. They had to count like mad to know exactly when to do the 'stabs'. It was very easy for them to miss cues, and very hard indeed to hit them as one, bang on.

Listen again to that verse with the horns in the background. Count the beats. Of the ten beats, the 'stabs' come first, halfway between the second and the third beat, on the fourth and seventh beat. They then begin the same routine, but second time round they have to begin a new phrase on the last beat of the verse. Not easy, if you try it. Think, too, of poor Ringo. His drumming had to be super-accurate, with all the walloping accents spot on. Lucky he was so good, really.

At one point I was saying to Sounds Incorporated something like, 'Look, we've got to do a triad of this, on E, followed by a triad on A.' John was watching all this with keen interest. 'Let me see now,' I went on to one of the sax players, 'you'll have to play a C sharp here, instead of an E—'

John interrupted me. 'George,' he said quizzically, 'you're giving them the wrong notes!'

'No I'm not, John; I'm really not,' I protested.

'I just heard you say they should play C sharp, but that's not the key we're in here, George.'

'No,' I explained, 'but they play a different note from your note. You see, when the baritone sax plays a C sharp it's really the same thing as your playing an E on the guitar.' He looked at me as if I was totally mad.

'But that's bloody stupid!' he said.

I suppose it is, really; but it had not occurred to him then that instruments could be in entirely different keys. I tried explaining that it was like tuning a guitar up to a different key, but he said, 'This is permanent, isn't it? These instruments are always in different keys.'

All I could do was shrug my shoulders: there was nothing to be done about it! 'Yes; it's just one of those facts of life, John,' I told him, laughing. 'We just have to cope with it.'

He didn't really want to learn about all the complications; as usual, John just wanted to get on with the recording. But he was astonished that people had to go through what he thought of as a time-wasting rigmarole.

To follow the sound of the 'Kellogg's' cockerel at the end of 'Good Morning', John had the idea of putting animal noises on it, and of putting these sounds in sequence. The idea was that we always had an animal that could swallow up the animal that came immediately before it. It was a bit like the old Burl Ives hit, which John would have known as a boy, 'The Spider And The Fly'. We used 'Volume 35: Animals and Bees' from EMI's sound effects library for our noises.

This was all great fun to do: rather like 'Revolution No. 9', later, or 'Tomorrow Never Knows', we had this wonderful panorama of sound in front of us to create and manipulate to our hearts' content. Mixing for stereo, later, I used to sit forward of the control panel, so that I was right inside the stereo triangle. In this position I could hear the sounds as I panned them, moving right across the imaginary landscape that was called up in me by the song.

The sound didn't travel from right to left, though: instead it sounded as though it were travelling up, and overhead. It was like listening to a rainbow of music arching over me. As the Beatles sang and played, and the animal sounds came in, I was watching a story unfolding in my mind.

I suddenly realized as I was pulling it together that the chicken noise we had dubbed on sounded really like the little bit before the reprise of 'Sgt. Pepper's Lonely Hearts Club Band', when the boys are tuning their guitars. So when I edited it together I turned the cluck-cluck of the chicken into the sound of a guitar string coming under tension as it is tuned, trying to mimic that twang, as near as I could. The chicken became the guitar.

It sounded great. It really welded the songs together. I couldn't congratulate myself too much on it, though, because it arrived all by itself – a stroke of luck. It just happened.

*

The Beatles had a trademark sound, the four of them playing and singing together; but they were not content to leave it at that. They kept changing, re-inventing themselves and their music. The Rolling Stones, on the other hand, never varied their sound much at all. Even the Beach Boys didn't introduce much variety into their basic formula. But as the Beatles grew up, musically, and particularly during the run-up to *Pepper*, every new track that came out was a fresh experience. They had a whole catalogue of identifiable sounds. They were not just one group, they were many. On *Pepper*, they were freewheeling.

The progression from the 'two guitars, bass and drums' formula of 'She Loves You' to the virtuoso musical collage that is *Pepper* is breathtakingly swift, when you look at it. From album to album, the Beatles made a quantum leap each time.

The first big departure from the standard rock 'n' roll line-up occurs with 'Yesterday', which was not performed by a group at all but by a string quartet accompanying a single acoustic guitar and a solo voice. Once the breakout had occurred, this process of continual experimentation and change, of musical and technical innovation, continued at top speed, through *Rubber Soul* and on into *Revolver*. By the time we got to that album there were some really weird things happening, like 'Tomorrow Never Knows'. This sounded as if there were no group there at all – and it still sounds contemporary. There are things in it that you would swear could come only from a 1990s synthesizer.

This diversity of expression really blossomed to its full extent on *Sgt. Pepper*. Take the classicism of 'She's Leaving Home', where you have a harp, a string octet and a couple of voices – no rhythm, no guitar; or the riotous inventiveness of 'Mr. Kite', with its bass harmonicas, funny cut-up tapes in the background, distorted organ sounds – which is really no longer very much like a traditional pop group at all. 'Sgt. Pepper' itself, the title song, that is, was the most identifiably 'Beatles' sound, because it was clearly a rock 'n' roll track of the kind the Beatles had been producing by the dozen. We even changed that, though, by setting out to make a much more 'live' sound, a sound that had not until then been satisfactorily captured, though many had tried.

Although it was produced in the studio, the 'Sgt. Pepper's Lonely Hearts Club Band' track, especially the reprise, does succeed in breaking out of its four walls, in capturing some of the energy of a live concert. And even though it was a rocker, it still made liberal use of classical instruments, most noticeably French horns. 'Within You Without You' was a complete departure again, a full foray into Indian music, what with its dilrubas, tambouras, sitars and tablas, combined uncannily with Western classical strings.

In the end *Pepper* was like a catalogue of the Beatles wares; it was as if they were saying, 'Look what we can give you, all these different things . . . '

The first album the Beatles recorded, *Please Please Me*, had them scrabbling to keep up with their success as a live act; it was a straightforward performance of their stage repertoire – a broadcast, more or less. We recorded the whole thing, all fourteen tracks, in a matter of hours. The only thought that went into it was: give the fans on record what they can hear on stage – as quickly as possible.

The albums as a whole developed from being collections of short rock 'n' roll tracks, some less than two minutes long, to songs that started saying a bit more. In most of those early songs, Lennon and McCartney were singing directly to the Female Fan, articulating her daydreams and probably their own. Most of the early lyrics feed this unrequited, fantasy relationship: 'Please Please Me', 'Love Me Do', 'I Want To Hold Your Hand', 'Hold Me Tight' . . . Nothing very subtle about that. Later on, in 1964, when they hit the USA, the Beatles started thinking more seriously about what their songs were saying.

By 1966 the Beatles had gone through the trauma of success, and had moved up several gears in the way they were writing songs – as had I in the way we were recording them. They were excited by the strides they were making as songwriters and recording artists, as well as by the technical possibilities opening up to them. The two albums immediately prior to *Pepper* – *Revolver* and *Rubber Soul* – both contain some of their best work. *Rubber Soul* still had the musical directness and simplicity of the preceding years, but the lyrics of the songs were becoming more interesting. John in particular started flagging messages in his songs, as he developed musically. *Rubber Soul* has a good example of this.

Judy and I were on a skiing holiday with John and Cynthia in

Switzerland when John began 'Norwegian Wood'. Sitting in the hotel bedroom one evening, he sang to us the embryo of this new song, which he finished later at Weybridge with Paul. I never thought of it as being malicious towards Cyn, but it obviously was: 'I once had a girl, or should I say, she once had me . . . ' He would sing it with a little quizzical look in his face, a sidelong glance at Cyn. Having got Cynthia pregnant at a very early age, he had been obliged to marry her. It was the done thing in those days, because if you didn't do it you were more or less damned and consigned to live for ever beyond the pale of decent British society. Harrumph!

He was happy enough then, though – it wasn't nasty – but there was an edge there, all the same. Ironic, tongue-in-cheek . . . It was a mental shrug at his circumstances. Later on, John said 'Norwegian Wood' was about an extra-marital affair he was having at the time; it was his way of 'confessing' to Cynthia without telling her outright. You can hear Bob Dylan in there, on that one, telling it like it is.

By the time *Revolver* came along we were into an era of trying things out like mad in the studio, an era of almost continuous technological experimentation. This went so far that on one occasion Geoff Emerick put a microphone in a bowl of water to see what it would sound like when you sang into the bowl. Needless to say, it ruined an expensive mike, and Geoff nearly got himself fired for it!

New technology: that was the key. It wasn't so much that I was trying to please the Beatles, to enact their experimental ideas, though that was always a priority. My own specialities were beginnings and endings, and solos. If they presented me with a song, I would start thinking about how to arrange it so that it got off to a cracking start, had something interesting going on in the middle, and went out with a big bang. You can only sing a pop song through once, and this is not generally long enough, so you need maybe a middle eight, a guitar solo, a repeated chorus, and an outro. A pretty simple formula really, but they relied on me to do it.

Increasingly, that simple formula became inadequate. 'Rain' needed something on the playout, to give it a lift; so I took one of John's phrases he had sung and turned it round, realizing that musically it would fit – the line would fit the chords – and that it might sound intriguing. I pasted it on, and it sounded good. That simple reversal, together with the drone of the tamboura, gave the song a kind of mystical feel that was very different from our other stuff to date. John flipped when he heard it, and so did Paul: they wanted everything recorded backwards after that!

But it is another song, recorded almost at the same time as 'Rain', that shows how far the Beatles had come in four short years. This song, 'Tomorrow Never Knows', picks up the hint of the mystic in 'Rain' and really runs with it. For a start, the lyrics were pinched from the *Tibetan Book of the Dead* (the Dr Timothy Leary edition), which John was reading at the time. Then George was anxious to use his newly acquired knowledge of Indian music, so we used a tamboura on it. The tamboura is like a sitar, but has an even greater number of tuned strings, in octaves and fifths, which the player strokes continuously to give a never-ending, mesmeric resonation of sounds. The fluctuation of the harmonics gave you this lovely silky, dreamy background sound, the musical equivalent of the joss-stick. We used that as eardrum filler, while Ringo thumped a very heavy off-beat on his bass drum, which had a big woollen jumper stuffed into it by Geoff Emerick to deaden the sound.

'Tomorrow Never Knows' was the first song to be recorded for *Revolver*. The basic rhythm track was made up of a very definite rock drumbeat from Ringo, plus the tamboura drone, with its res-onating strings. We built up a 'pad' of tamboura sounds, to get continuous wafting overtones of that single drone. On top of these two main elements, which are the basis of the song, we added the voice. That vocal. True to form, John wanted me to 'do something with it'. 'I want it to sound,' he said, 'as if I'm singing from the top of a hill; I want to sound like a Buddhist monk, singing from the top of a mountain. Like the Dalai Lama. Distant, but I still want to hear it.' He wanted to make real the voice he had heard inside his head when he was reading the book. Well, that wasn't asking much, now was it?

Apart from the *Tibetan Book of the Dead*, the exotic sound of the tamboura, and John wanting to sound like a mystical zombie, there was still more of the weird and wonderful to come on this song, and it came from Paul. Paul was very much into what we called the avant-garde in those days: modern art, literature, modern music by the likes of John Cage, Stockhausen – the things he heard in the fruitful environment provided by the family Asher. The Ashers, who took Paul in when he started going out with Jane, were very perceptive people, highly intelligent and very musical. Although no one could ever say they had any taste for the avant-garde, they encouraged Paul in his musical self-education to experiment and to be free, musically, if he felt like it.

As an aid to better song writing Paul had a couple of Brennell tape-recorders at home. He discovered that by taking off the erase head, and using only the record head, any sound you care to make will record as normal and will not erase next time round. Instead, that sound will go past the replay head and be recorded again, and again and again, until it saturates the tape. If you play that sound back, it comes out sounding nothing whatsoever like the noise you started off with (which was obviously highly desirable, if you were a Beatle!). Paul constructed all these 'loops' of tape with these funny, distorted, dense little noises on them. He told the others, and they, too, took the wipe heads off their recorders and started constructing loops of taped gibberish.

They would all bring me in these loops, like cats bringing in sparrows. I would listen to them, play them at different speeds, backwards and forwards, at three-and-three-quarters, seven-and-a-half or fifteen feet per second, and select liberally from them. From the thirty or so tapes they brought in, I selected sixteen loops I liked, each about six seconds long, to use on 'Tomorrow Never Knows'.

'We've got our track,' I said. 'We've got the rhythm, we've got the tamboura drone, we've got John's voice, that's the basis. Now we're going to decorate it with these "bits and pieces". What we'll do is use the recording console like an organ. We'll have all these loops being played, at the same time, continuously. We can't cope with sixteen, but we can cope with about eight.' We had an eight-track mixing desk – which was a bit ironic, since our tape recorders could only hold four tracks apiece, as I've already explained.

What I had to do then was find eight tape-recorders that could each play a tape-loop. So I took over EMI. I went to every room in the Abbey Road building and said, 'Look, I want a tape-machine, with a guy standing by it playing this loop of tape here continuously. And to keep it on the heads, the operator will need a pencil, to maintain his own particular loop of tape on tension.'

The tape-recording machines in those days were enormous, big BTR3s. Once one was in place, it could not easily be moved. So we had white-coated operatives standing all over Abbey Road, on every floor of the building, each in front of a BTR3 with a pencil stuck in a small loop of tape. Each continuous loop was fed through Abbey Road's internal jack plug patching system, down through the intervening walls and floors, out into our studio, and plugged into my mixing console. By raising a fader, I would hear a particular loop going round and round, held in position by a man in a white coat several floors away, playing its cacophony continuously for ever and ever. Talk about hi-tech!

When we came to mix the song, then, all we had to do was bring up one fader at a time, and use the mixing-desk's pan-pot to put it anywhere in 'the screen' (that is, to position it anywhere we wanted in the stereo spectrum, left to right). We all thought this was great fun. 'I know,' I said. 'Why don't we all mix the song at the same time?'

So that is what we did. Paul would have a couple of faders to play with, Ringo and George might have a couple, I would be doing the panning and telling them when they were overdoing it, and that's how we got our melange of weird and wonderful sounds on 'Tomorrow Never Knows'. Geoff Emerick was keeping a general eye on the meters to make sure no one was doing anything excessive. Halfway through we got bored with the tapes we'd been using, so we took those ones off and put on the other eight for the rest of the song.

While all this was going on we had John's voice rolling away in the background. To make him sound like a Buddhist monk, his dearest wish at that moment, we had put his voice through the Leslie loudspeaker of our Hammond organ. A Leslie speaker rotates at different speeds inside the cabinet of a Lowry organ. You can make the speaker rotate faster or slower by depressing a pedal. It gives a kind of doppler, or 'wah-wah' effect. We put his voice into that speaker, 87 seconds into the song, then recorded it through another microphone placed outside the Leslie speaker. It gave this weird impression of a voice that was somehow pulsating, far-off and altogether singular, as he wished.

John was pleased as Punch with that; he thought it was great. In fact, he was so keen on it that Geoff Emerick suggested the reverse idea: that we suspend John upside down from a piece of rope and spin him round while he was singing, instead of rotating the speaker! Even John wouldn't take things quite that far, though.

It was a strange track, great fun to do, and one from an album that gave a kick-start to the kind of experimental recording we would be doing later, on *Pepper*. It is also the one track, of all the songs the Beatles did, that could never be reproduced: it would be impossible to go back now and mix exactly the same thing: the 'happening' of the tape loops, inserted as we all swung off the levers on the faders willy-nilly, was a random event. *Revolver* was the first album from which no song was ever performed; the Beatles took on their last tour after completing that album, but they never performed a track from it live. Normally they would always be very anxious to perform hits from their latest, but they knew very well that the tracks on *Revolver* were getting intricate, to say the least, and that they couldn't do them on stage.

They certainly couldn't do 'Tomorrow Never Knows' with the technology we had then; they couldn't even do 'Eleanor Rigby' – how could they incorporate the strings? So they never bothered: they just trotted out the same old pot-boilers when they had to: 'Day Tripper', 'I Feel Fine', 'I Wanna Be Your Man' . . . This was the other side of *Pepper*; it grew naturally out of *Revolver*, continuing and developing from there.

The Beatles and I were helped in our madcap schemes by Ken Townsend, now managing director of Abbey Road studios, then a backroom engineer who was very enthusiastic about our experiments. It was Ken who dreamed up an early form of double-tracking called Artificial Double Tracking, or ADT, based on frequency control: the two tape-machines used for the double-tracking were not driven from mains electricity but from a generator which put out a particular frequency, the same one for both tape-recorders, so that the master track and the copying track stayed more or less locked together. Again, John was very pleased with what this could do to his voice, and demanded to know how it worked. I started to explain, and then noticed his eyes glazing over.

So I thought I would blind him with science. Taking a leaf out of Professor Stanley Unwin's book, I explained carefully to John that the recording of his voice was specially treated with a 'double-bifurcated sploshing flange. It doubles your voice, John . . . ' He

82

eventually realized I was having him on, but forever afterwards he would say, 'George, shall we flange the voice here?'

Many years later I was in America and I heard the phrase used by a local recording engineer. 'Where did that word come from?' I asked him. 'Oh,' he replied, 'it's an effect you can get by pushing your thumb on the flange of the tape reel . . . ' Whatever he liked to think, I reckon! You can now buy 'flange boxes' for guitar effects, and so on.

As the Beatles began kicking over the traces of popular musical conventions, it gave me the freedom to do more of what I enjoyed: experimenting, building sound-pictures, creating a whole atmosphere for a song, all the things I'd always loved doing anyway. It was a very happy marriage. I didn't have to ask anyone's permission: that was the wonderful thing, that autonomy, that power. As long as the five of us agreed, everyone else could go hang!

Creating atmosphere and sound-pictures . . . that was my bag. I did a lot of it before the Beatles even came along. In 1962 Parlophone issued a single called: 'Time Beat/Waltz In Orbit', a compilation of electronic sounds, composed by a certain 'Ray Cathode' – me!

Just along the road from us at Abbey Road, the BBC had set up an experimental sound department, called the Radiophonics Workshop. I was fascinated, and got to know some of the engineers down there: people who spent their entire time cooking up freaky sounds, with whatever they could lay their hands on. They had the (to them) standard equipment, of oscillators and variable speed tape machines, but they also indulged in quite a bit of concrete music. Milk bottles, bits of old piping . . . *Blue Peter* had nothing on these guys. Their greatest claim to fame was their collaboration with Ron Grainer, which brainstormed the amazing theme music for *Doctor Who*.

Ray Cathode came about because I decided to add a few live musicians to a rhythmic track of pure, synthetic sound the Workshop had dreamed up. It was a resounding flop. But an interesting flop . . . Something to learn from, anyway! The Peter Sellers tracks I recorded were also exercises in building up sound-pictures. On one track, for example, Peter played at being a group of critics, which meant we had to create five different Peters, each with a different voice. Recording in stereo, we had one voice in the middle and two on each side, giving the illusion of a 'panel' of them talking to one another.

Irene Handl and Sellers did a sketch together called 'Shadows in the Grass', all in the studio, with very little completed script, the basic idea being that a silly old woman walking in the park is gradually seduced by a wily Frenchman. I edited the fifteen minutes of their ad-libbing down to seven minutes, took out the pauses, then overdubbed things like the crunching of feet on gravel, the faint hum of traffic in the distance, a little bit of birdsong, a little bit of rustling of leaves. When we listened back to it, the illusion that we were listening to two people walking through a park was remarkable, with just these few little touches.

It was Debussy's *L'après-midi d'un faune* that started me off down this particular road. I heard it for the first time when I was fifteen, in my school hall, performed by the BBC Symphony Orchestra with Adrian Boult conducting. Sitting there, listening, I started seeing these images: the drowsy buzz of a summer wood, the dapple of light and shade, the deer and the other animals browsing in the summer heat. It made me realize that the fences we put up between 'art' and 'music' could be broken down, that crossover might sometimes be possible. We certainly tried to do something of that on *Pepper*.

By the time of *Pepper*, then, the Beatles had immense power at Abbey Road. So did I. They used to ask for the impossible, and sometimes they would get it. At the beginning of their recording career, I used to boss them about – especially for the first year or so. By the time we got to *Pepper*, though, that had all changed: I was very much the collaborator. Their ideas were coming through thick and fast, and they were brilliant. All I did was help make them real.

9 February 1967: 'And it really doesn't matter if I'm wrong I'm right . . .'

Paul knew exactly where he was going with 'Fixing A Hole'. As a result, it was one of the fastest tracks we recorded, in an album of thirteen songs that took some five months to complete.

It took only two days. It's a very simply constructed song, built around a harpsichord and a bass guitar. Even before we got into the studio, Paul had decided to use a harpsichord as the mainstay of his rhythm; even so, the bass line is more important than the harpsichord line. Paul had to play bass guitar on it, because nobody could (or can) play that instrument quite like him. That meant someone else was going to have to play keyboards. This was unusual, because Paul always liked to play his own keyboards on his own compositions. The part of honorary stand-in keyboard player to the greatest group in the world was offered to me. It wasn't too difficult, and it didn't seem likely to tax my non-virtuoso technique too much.

Paul let rip with a superb and melodic bass line – something that was rapidly becoming a characteristic of his song-writing style. He used the instrument like a voice: he was never content just to use the dominant and tonic – the normal plodding sequences of a bass – as many others did. He wanted to make that bass sing. Whenever he had something to say, he said it most eloquently using the instrument he loved the best.

Curiously enough, in the beginning Paul never really wanted to play bass. He became the Beatles' bassist only when there was no one else to do it. Stuart Sutcliffe, the band's original bassist, was really an artist, not a musician, and he was never quite up to the job as a bass player. When he died, in 1962, someone had to take on the role.

Of all the Beatles, Paul was the most talented musician. When I first met him he could not play the piano at all. It was a very short time indeed from then to 'Lady Madonna', which is a very complicated and extremely good piano track played entirely by Paul, and a measure of his great musicianship. Paul could play the drums, technically, better than any of the others, including Ringo (although he could never get anything like the distinctive sound Ringo got from his kit). So, by default, Paul took over the most difficult instrument to play with any originality in a rock 'n' roll band: the bass guitar.

'Fixing A Hole' was the first time we went outside Abbey Road studios to record during *Sgt. Pepper*. Quite often Paul had a song suddenly come to him, and while it was fresh in his mind he would want to crystallize it. He could not write music, so apart from scribbling down the lyrics and noting a few chord changes underneath, there was no other way for him to be sure of grabbing the song while it was there in his head, other than by recording it. A Walkman would have come in useful!

Normally, Abbey Road moved heaven and earth to accommodate the Beatles in their hour of need. Nevertheless, the studios and staff could hardly be kept idle in case a Beatle had a flash of inspiration. Although there had been talk of finally building a special recording studio solely for the Beatles – grabbing studio reservation ahead of any others was becoming a bit of an embarrassment – nothing had come of it. It so happened that all the studios were in use that particular night, 9 February: there was no room for them at the inn. We had to find a studio, and quickly, while Paul had the urge. The one we found, Regent Sound in Tottenham Court Road, was little more than a demonstration studio, in the heart of Tin Pan Alley. It was a low-ceilinged, boxy little room with a low-ceilinged boxy little sound to it.

On top of this, we weren't allowed to take our engineers with us: Geoff Emerick was employed by Abbey Road in those days and contractually prevented from recording elsewhere. A man called Adrian Ibbetson was head of Regent Sound then, so he did the recording.

We followed the same formula as usual, putting the rhythm – in this case harpsichord, bass and drums – on to Track 1. Track 2 carried lead guitar, a lengthy and very good solo from George.

George had his guitar volume and both bass and top tone controls up very high. Vocals and rhythm guitar went on to Track 3 (together!). We then put backing vocals on Track 4, which was as far as we got that night. Paul took home a lacquer – a rough mix of the song on acetate disc – so that he could listen to it and think about it overnight.

We picked up 'Fixing A Hole' about two weeks later, on 21 February, on home ground once more at Abbey Road. Geoff Emerick made a reduction mix of the Regent Sound Take 2. This new mix-down was labelled Take 3. The song was then ready for mastering. This all sounds a bit complicated, as always, but it wasn't: after only two sessions we had finished the song.

Compositions change with the instrument you are writing with. No pianist, for example, could ever have written 'I Feel Fine'. That opening riff, which is the cornerstone of the song, is a guitar lick if ever you heard one. It is pretty obvious that John, who was a guitarist and not really much of anything else, fooled around for hours until he stumbled upon this little phrase, which he thought was great. Generally, by listening to a song, you can work out whether it was written by a guitarist or a pianist – or any other type of 'ist'.

'Fixing A Hole' is very recognizably a keyboard song. You can see the three-finger piano chords underpinning its structure. Those basic triads are the platform on which the lead voice, Paul's voice, and the bass guitar, were overlaid.

John would always have a pretty good idea of where he wanted to get to with a song, too. He would have an image in his mind, but he would not necessarily have a very good idea of how to get there, in practical terms. Paul was much more articulate about what he wanted, much more focused. John would tell me what kind of mood he wanted on the song, whereas Paul would ask for a cello, say, or a trumpet at a certain point. Then, at the end of everything, John would be unhappy that he had not quite got the final result he wanted.

In a way, *Sgt. Pepper* is a utopia. John was a super-realist, but at the same time he was always looking for instant utopias. He was a paradox. He never heard, in real life, what he dreamed he could hear. What we heard was something of what he wanted, interpreted by me and the rest of the Beatles, but a something that always fell short of his own image of perfection. And that, in a way, is perhaps a measure of my failure.

At the same time, a small part of me is sceptical of all this, because I know how easy it is to fool oneself with the imagination, with dreams. I have often dreamt wonderful sounds but realized even in my dream that if I ever tried to make them real, on waking, they would not actually sound anything like as good. Perhaps, in reality, John did get as near as he could to making his musical dreams come true; we'll never know.

To John, the recording process was like the difference between a good lithograph and the original painting that is locked away in a vault somewhere, and never seen. I hope that wherever he is now his dreams are being realized – the painting and not the pale imitation.

My professional life, during the Beatle years, had, of course, one overriding purpose: to make sure the Beatles got what they wanted. I remember a lovely phrase I once heard in a French film, whose title I cannot remember: 'Music is dreams.'

It was their dreams we were realizing: nothing more or less. Music requires mechanics, people banging, or blowing, or scraping, or strumming; but in the end it is intangible, it is dreams. You can't get hold of music, you cannot look at it. You may think you can look at it by picking up a score, but that is just a piece of paper. Music does not exist without a pair of serviceable ears, and time. That is why I think it is the most wonderful art of all – why I get so ecstatic about it. Above all other things, music needs time.

CHAPTER TEN

17 February 1967:
'A splendid time is
guaranteed for all . . .'

'Being For The Benefit Of Mr. Kite' is another good example of the way John Lennon would write directly from his life, transmuting and transmogrifying into song what was happening to him day to day. At the end of January 1967, the Beatles were shooting a promotional film in Knole Park, near Sevenoaks, Kent, for their new 'Strawberry Fields Forever'/'Penny Lane' double-A-sided single. (In a way, this film is one of the very first pop videos ever made.) Ever the magpie, John had been browsing in a Sevenoaks antique shop and had come across an old Victorian poster. It advertised a circus that actually took place, in 1843, in a field near Rochdale, Lancashire. He bought it on the spot, and gave it pride of place in his entrance hall in Weybridge.

Obviously the events shown on the poster fired his imagination, and inspired him and Paul to write the song that was to become such a fundamental part of *Pepper*. All the names in the song are there, on that ageing bit of vellum: the Henderson Twins, Pablo Fanques, Mr Kite . . . as are most of the lyrics. 'I'd love to be able to get across all the effects of a really colourful circus,' John told me. 'The acrobats in their tights, the smell of the animals, the merry-go-rounds. I want to smell the sawdust, George.' How to achieve that? How to get all that with a microphone or two in a North London studio?

John came to me initially with his acoustic guitar, playing and singing through the new song to give us both a rough idea of what we were dealing with. Then we discussed what he wanted to do with the song eventually. We knew pretty much from the start what we were out to get, in terms of a general idea; we tried always to work in this way. Very rarely did we waste time groping in the dark. We were always looking to bring something new to the music, but it had to be focused experimentation, and be very deliberate.

In the case of 'Being For The Benefit Of Mr. Kite' I knew it had to be a kind of hurdy-gurdy sound, that much was obvious; but I asked John if he had any ideas. He came up with a bizarre answer: 'I've always loved the sound of the music to that children's programme *The Magic Roundabout*. It's really simple, but it's great.' It was a very tooty kind of sound. John loved children's television programmes, he often watched them.

'Funny you should say that,' I replied. 'I had in mind the little organ in Disney's *Snow White*, the one the dwarfs had: a very pipy sound. The real equivalent, though, would be a steam organ, a calliope – what they have on carousels.'

If you go to a fair, the first thing you hear is the sound of the merry-go-round, against the background racket from the crowd. In the early days, those carousels with the horses going up and down were powered by steam, and so, therefore, were their organ-pipes. I started looking for steam organs. They did still exist in 1967. I got really excited, thinking that we could get one and play the accompaniment on that – great! I did a little research, though, and found out that the fairground organs were rather like pianolas: the sequence of the notes was determined by a series of punched cards that went over drums, which in turn opened or closed certain stops.

It was going to be very difficult to make up an original punched card of our own, and it would take up a lot of time. John thought I should get one; after all, the Beatles were famous for leaving no stone unturned in achieving the sound they were after, and the idea of importing a huge steam organ into Abbey Road appealed to their eccentric natures enormously!

I, however, had to be more practical; manufacturing our own calliope for a single track just wasn't on. I had a better idea: I could probably use existing recordings. I gathered up all the recordings of steam organs I could find, but I quickly ran into a major problem. They were almost all military marches: Sousa's 'Stars and Stripes Forever' . . . 'Blaze Away', that kind of thing! Useless for the atmosphere we wanted. Or was it? I went back to John and said, 'What we should do is create a special backing track with organs and mouth-organs – a pumping kind of sound.' We began by using just the harmonium, the big beast that was part of the furniture at Abbey Road. This was the beginning: then we had to overlay the special effects using a Hammond and a Lowry organ, together with our well-beloved roadie, Mal Evans, playing a massive bass harmonica. John and I had great fun, giggling helplessly as we tried to sort out the organ runs and interrupting one another.

When it got to the bit after the line 'And of course, Henry the Horse dances the waltz . . . ' John wanted the music to swirl round and round, and carry you into a sequence of a horse dancing. I realized the way to do that would be to have a tremendous chromatic run up on an organ, which I would have to play: John couldn't play the piano that well. When it came down to doing it, though, neither could I! I was better, but I still couldn't do it fast enough for what we wanted to achieve. The only way I could do it was to slow the tape down to half speed, which allowed me to play the notes nice and slowly, at a pace I could manage.

It is a fact of physics that if you slow the tape down to half speed, then the frequencies are halved, and the sound drops down an octave lower exactly. I duly played the notes an octave down, recording them at that speed, then on playback speeded the tape back up to normal. Eureka! It worked!

John did play along, on another organ – he did all the 'oompahpahs', while I did the swirly bits. And it sounded pretty good. But there was still something missing. I knew what it was: it was the calliope, the steam organ. There was no way round it. If we wanted that authentic fairground atmosphere, we had to have one.

I went back to all the recordings of marches and what-not I'd collected, and transferred them on to one tape. Again, a little bit of a brainwave was required. What, though? Finally, an idea came up. I selected two-minute segments of the taped music. Then I got hold of Geoff, who by this stage was more than my engineer on our extraordinary album, he was my co-conspirator. 'Geoff,' I said, 'we're going to try something here; I want you to cut that tape there up into sections that are roughly fifteen inches long.' Geoff reached for his scissors and began snipping.

In no time at all we had a small pyramid of worm-like tape fragments piled up on the floor at our feet. 'Now,' I said, 'pick them all up and fling them into the air!' He looked at me. Naturally, he thought I'd gone mad.

It was a wonderful moment – it snowed pieces of tape all over the control room. I had an instant flashback to the day I was demobbed out of the Fleet Air Arm in 1947. The last thing the Navy gave me was my gratuity of £260, all in single pound notes. It was the largest amount of money I had ever had. When I arrived home, the first thing I did was to take out that wodge of massive old pound notes, fling them all over the room, and rush about trying to catch them. Wonderful!

'Now, pick 'em up and put them together again, and don't look at what you're doing,' I told Geoff. Strangely enough, Sod's Law being what it is, some of the pieces of tape went back together almost where they'd started. We got round that by turning anything that sounded like it might be in the correct sequence around and splicing it in back to front. In this peculiar way we made up a patchwork quilt of different parts of steam organ recordings, all in roughly one-second segments: lots of different pieces whirling around. When I listened to them, they formed a chaotic mass of sound: it was impossible to identify the tunes they had come from; but it was unmistakably a steam organ. Perfect! There was the fairground atmosphere we had been looking for. John was thrilled to bits with it.

All the noises in a fairground recede into the distance when you are talking to somebody nearby, so the sound of the steam organs had to be subliminal. I had to be sure to keep them audible, but well in the background. That edited tape of steam organs still exists at Abbey Road today, separate from the four-track master tapes.

As to the 'Kite' recording process itself, that began on the evening of 17 February 1967, a Friday. As so often, we began by filling up our four available tracks with the basic rhythm to the song.

TRACK 1: bass guitar – Paul
TRACK 2: guide vocal – John
TRACK 3: drums – Ringo
TRACK 4: harmonium – me

I remember only too well pumping away with my feet at that bloody harmonium for hour after hour, trying to get it right, and being absolutely knackered, heart going at about 130 beats to the minute. It was like climbing up a steep flight of stairs non-stop. We would complete a take, I'd heave a sigh of relief, mop my sweaty brow, and then the dreaded call would come from John: 'I wouldn't mind doing that again, George. You all right there?' The harmonium was a good idea, though, because it established a vaguely circusy atmosphere to the song straight off.

After we laid down the four basic rhythm tracks you can hear John saying in an ironic voice, 'And after this we'll have the Massed Alberts, won't we, George?' The 'Massed Alberts' were, or was, a bizarre and eccentric English comedy act, a duo I had recorded in the early days along with Spike Milligan. The Alberts ran newspaper delivery vans during the day, to make a living, and in the evening put on comedy performances entitled, 'An Evening of British Rubbish', and so on, in various little theatres around the land. One of the Alberts played the trumpet rather badly, which is what John meant by his comment: it was time to add on 'the clever stuff', the brass.

That night we transferred those original four tracks to a new tape. By combining the bass guitar and harmonium on Track 1 of the new tape, and transferring the drums to Track 2, we were left with two open tracks. We ditched John's original guide vocal, and added his new lead vocal to Track 4. Not wishing to waste a second of recording space, we added more organ in the gaps on that vocal track. Our last empty track, Track 3, received all the additional 'whirligig' organ sounds we had concocted, some of it recorded at a very fast fifty-six-and-a-half cycles, to get the weird high-pitched sound we wanted. Other bits we recorded very slowly, at seven-and-a-half feet per second, because I could not play the organ fast enough, as I explained above. We completed recording on the Monday, again working seven hours right through into the small hours.

And there was 'Mr. Kite'.

If you listen to the music of the twenties and thirties, it has a certain sound to it; it's partly the song that you like, and it's partly the way it was recorded, the tube amplifiers in the boards, how the microphone

93

sounded in those days, all that kind of atmosphere. It becomes like a little period piece, just like a piece of furniture of a given period, it has its own charm. You wouldn't want to hear the Beatles doing Mr. Kite on a forty-eight-track machine, it wouldn't have the same charm.

— George Harrison, *South Bank Show*

CHAPTER ELEVEN

23 February 1967: 'Where would I be without you?'

... it doesn't have to be us, it doesn't have to be the kind of song you want to write, it could be the kind of song they might want to write ... you could write a song about Lovely Rita, meter maid ... Paul McCartney might not have ... but these people could, so it was very liberating and that's how we looked at the whole thing. — Paul, *South Bank Show*

It seemed as though we were going to record 'Lovely Rita' in a leap and a bound when we first began working on it, much as we had done with 'Fixing A Hole'. We laid down four basic takes, Takes 3, 4, 5 and 6 all being false starts. Take 8 was marked as the best take of the night.

TRACK 1: George Harrison on acoustic and slide guitars (the very striking 'swoop up' at the beginning of the song is produced by George on slide guitar).

TRACK 2: John on a second acoustic guitar

TRACK 3: Ringo playing drums

TRACK 4: Paul on piano, with tape echo on the piano

We reduced those four tracks down to the first track of a second tape, labelled Track 9. This reduction was recorded at a lower speed than normal, forty-eight-and-three-quarter cycles, as we were experimenting with tape speed again. That same night we laid down Paul's bass guitar track. We had worked through from 7 p.m. on the 23rd until 4 a.m. the next morning.

Even though we had worked so long and so late, we were back in the studio the next evening at seven. Now we set to on Paul's vocals, with the tape-machine running at forty-six-and-a-half cycles, so that his voice sounded faster and higher in pitch on replay at the normal speed. At this stage the song had a much longer piano introduction, which we cut down later. Although we did nothing other than work on the vocals that night, we still ended up working until 1.15 in the morning.

We then left 'Lovely Rita' to her own devices for a couple of weeks, until 7 March. That evening we recorded down John's and Paul's backing vocals, on Track 4, with heavy tape echo on the voices. There was a lot of off-the-cuff fooling around, and we even resorted to a choir of paper and combs, as a mock brass section. They all blew through combs covered with regulation-issue EMI toilet paper, to create a bizarre, kazoo-like sound. George complained frequently to the EMI management about the horrible slippery hardness of its loo paper. (Each sheet had the legend 'Property of EMI' stamped across it!) He said it was OK for wrapping round a comb and blowing through, but as to using it for what it was intended, you could forget it! (The tissue issue finally had to get to board level before it could be sorted out, and a better class of toilet paper was eventually installed for our use!)

A selection of these weird and wonderful noises made by John, with a little help from the others, was to finish up on the play-out of the song.

We still weren't finished with the lovely lady: she had a big hole in the middle of her where a solo ought to be. 'Big' George (that's me) was elected to play said solo, which we did on 21 March. I wanted a rippling honky-tonk piano sound, and got this by slowing the tape speed down to forty-one-and-a-quarter cycles, thereby reducing the pitch by three semitones. That way I was able to play the notes I wanted at a reasonable speed. When we brought the solo back up to normal speed again it sounded quite fast, and pretty good. Even better, it still sounded like a piano and not like a harpsichord, as double-speed piano tends to do.

I also altered the sound of my piano on that solo by putting a spot of 'wow' on it. A very bad recording of a piano has a wobbly, wowing quality on the notes, which is a sound often produced by old tape-recorders. All the tape machines at EMI were top-line, however. How to destroy them? I put a tiny piece of editing tape on the capstan, which lifted the tape about a millimetre clear as it went over the roller. This put a bit of strain on the tape, making it oscillate and stretch just that little bit as it went round past the head. The effect was to give the piano the old-fashioned honky-tonk sound I was looking for.

This little trick saved the day for us. Although the Beatles had not themselves come up with anything for the middle eight of the song, they were less than thrilled by my piano solo idea. Paul had asked me to play through the solo when I first made the suggestion, but I was too embarrassed to do it live. He did like the finished product, though!

The song was finished, but it had no clear ending. It just petered out. When they were adding their backing vocals, the boys were spurred on by the heavy tape echo they could hear in their cans, and started fooling around with it. One sound would lead to another. So they would be panting like super-heated mongrels, moaning, cha-cha-cha-ing, clicking their tongues, and making all sorts of strange noises. John always loved messing around like that. (A memorable track that was to come much later, the seminal rocker 'Come Together' on *Abbey Road*, was virtually built around John's ad-lib vocal sounds.)

The anarchy that crept into the recording of 'Lovely Rita' was the beginning of the undisciplined, sometimes self-indulgent way of working that became a bit boring during *Magical Mystery Tour*. Boring, that is, for those of us who were not Beatles! Letting your hair down now and again and having a good muck about is a nice idea; but 'freedom' does not automatically confer brilliance.

Some people swear by 'Lovely Rita'. I have always found her company a little tedious. Perhaps I've suffered too often at the hands of the ladies with yellow bands round their hats!

I was hopping about on the piano playing in Liverpool when someone told me that in America they call parking-meter women 'meter maids'. I thought that was great, and it got to 'Rita Meter Maid' and I was thinking vaguely that it should be a hate song: 'You took my car away and I'm so blue today . . . ' And you wouldn't be liking her; but then I thought it would be better to love her, and if she was very freaky too, like a military man, with a bag on her shoulder. A foot stomper, but nice. – Paul, *South Bank Show*

Had John never met Paul, and vice versa. I firmly believe that neither of them would have turned out to be the great songwriters that they were. They would have been good, but not blisteringly great, as millions of us think they are. Each had a tremendous influence on the other, which neither of them consciously realized.

John would probably have ended up as a sort of Lou Reed or Dylan figure, singing protest songs in one form or another. Paul would probably have written safe, acceptable, soft, melodic songs, lacking the acidity he absorbed from John.

The famous hyperbole of *The Times* newspaper's music critic, who likened the Beatles to Schubert, speaking in glowing terms of 'pan diatonic clusters' in their music was, I agree, a bit over the top. It was not all that far off, though. Paul McCartney has a sense of structure in his compositions that very few popular songwriters have ever had. He instinctively had much more musicianship in him than any of the others did: Paul had the makings of a great composer.

Comparing Paul with someone like Andrew Lloyd Webber, for example, his qualities were immediately apparent. His basic raw material had a stronger simplicity than even the songs of that excellent writer. His output was more varied, and of course, in terms of pure songwriting he has been far more prolific. Mind you, he did have the advantage of having a pretty good band around to plug his efforts! I do believe that if Paul had been taught music and learned more about orchestration he could have ended up writing even better stage musicals than Lloyd Webber, if that is possible.

All the same, Andrew is a peerless composer for the theatre as Paul is in popular song, and they have both done very nicely, thank you.

In the early days my role was to tidy things up, musically – to put songs into some sort of perspective. (I would also give a commercial estimate of their worth.) I might take a phrase out of the middle of 'Can't Buy Me Love', for example, pointing out that the phrase should have started the song, or, as on 'Please Please Me', say 'Speed it up, mucho; that's all it needs, really . . . '

I think John learned from this kind of input. He learned a whole lot more from Paul, though: musical structure; organization in his song writing; how to make a song telling. He also learned the value of a good 'hook' – the catchy bit, for example the guitar riff that starts 'Day Tripper', the harmonica from 'Love Me Do'.

Paul was able to cut through the garbage and clearly present the essence of a good tune, with good harmonies. Yet he never fell back upon the conventional clichés of song writing. He would forever be coming up with a little musical twist that made a song, or a phrase, severely more interesting to listen to. 'The Fool On The Hill' has a basic melody, but at the end of what would, conventionally, have been the verse, the song does not stop, to mark the transition into the chorus. The 'verse' section flows on, seamlessly, effortlessly, unnoticeably, into the next element:

> And he doesn't know the answer,
> But the fool on the hill,
> Sees the sun going down . . .

Nobody else would have thought of this. It is a good example of Paul's lateral thinking, a touch of genius.

The attention-span of the listener governs the success of any piece of music. I realized this when I had John home to supper one night. I made him sit through Ravel's *Daphnis and Chloë* (Suite No. 2), which I think has to be one of the most beautiful pieces of music ever written: the perfect demonstration of an ideal orchestration. It takes about ten minutes, but ten minutes is a long time if you can't get into it.

John turned to me at the end and said: 'Yes, I know what you're getting at; but I couldn't really understand the tune.'

'But it's a wonderful tune . . .'

'Yes,' said John, 'but I'd forgotten how the beginning was by the time we got to the end.'

If you didn't hook John's attention within a few seconds, you lost him. I am afraid this is true of many listeners today – he was just a bit ahead of his time. Nowadays the pace created by technology – television, video games, computers – makes it increasingly difficult for people to assimilate some of the more subtle, longer passages of classical music.

CHAPTER TWELVE

28 February 1967:
'The girl with kaleidoscope
eyes ...'

The only problem with uncharted territory is that you can occasionally get lost in it; and lost we certainly got during the making of *Pepper*. We were dealing with a completely different class of song, experimenting technically all the time; there were complex tunes and harmonies to be worked on and worked out. Where nowadays a band might try things out using nothing more sophisticated than a Walkman, a toy like that would have been the ultimate in sophisticated technology for us. If we wanted to try a few things out, we had to use the whole of Abbey Road! The technical staff had to be on hand when we were kicking a song around, in case any of the Beatles struck a rich vein and wanted to lay something down. It was well known among the Abbey Road engineers that it was wonderful working with the Beatles, and making great sounds, but that it was equally unwonderful not working, sitting around and getting bored.

Trying to stay awake and alert while genius sorts itself out can be a major challenge! It was not only the engineers who suffered the tedium of attending on creative genius – I had to be there, too. And last but not least, all the Beatles had to be there, even if some of them were not directly involved. When he was asked what he remembers best about the recording of the album, Ringo replied: 'The biggest memory I have of *Sgt. Pepper* is that I learned to play chess.'

Ringo listened very carefully to what was happening on any song in progress, all the same. He was critical, in the same way that I could be critical, of what the others were doing, and not afraid to voice that criticism. He would suddenly say to John, 'John, that's crap,' whereupon John would look up over his glasses, and murmur, 'Oh really?' and change it. Either that or he'd make a rude remark back, and *then* change whatever it was that Ringo had picked up on.

Paul also took a great deal of notice of what Ringo said. He was a very effective guide, musically speaking; he had a good ear. Although he might not always have had all that much to do, you could never forget that he was a major part of the group.

On 28 February we started working on something at seven o'clock in the evening. It was something intangible: something we couldn't quite get at. We went right on working for eight hours, going home at three in the morning.

We still hadn't recorded a thing, except the odd stray line.

At seven o'clock on the evening of 1 March we started recording again, and finally laid down a first take, hardly more than a run-through, with the track layout looking like this:

TRACK 1: acoustic guitar – George

piano – me

TRACK 2: Lowry organ – Paul

TRACK 3: drums – Ringo

TRACK 4: guide vocal – John (very simple, with tape echo)

We had the rhythm – no voice. But this was special. This simple outline was eventually to become 'Lucy In The Sky With Diamonds'.

By the time we reached Take 7, everyone knew the song. I wanted to finish the backing as near as I could that night, so I wiped John's guide vocal and overdubbed a tamboura drone, with George, on to track four. By two-thirty in the morning we had a serviceable backing track.

For the introduction to the vocal we used a Lowry organ. The bell-like sound we got from it on 'Lucy' would have been extremely difficult to extract from a Hammond. The Hammond was the Rolls-Royce of the organ world then; it was used everywhere – remember 'A Whiter Shade Of Pale'? You could even find Hammonds at the end of English seaside piers, like the huge Wurlitzers that rose up slowly through the cinema floor, in the old days, before the main feature started.

It usually came equipped with a row of foot-pedals, to help you achieve anything from a cathedral-like bellow to a fairground toot. Despite its huge flexibility, however, the Hammond could not produce that spring-clear but slightly quavering note – the unique watery clarity we were looking for.

The Lowry was a much smaller and simpler instrument, with a series of pre-set stops that peeped out a more limited series of sounds. If anything, it was more like a modern-day synthesizer than a conventional organ. The great thing about the Lowry was that, whereas with the Hammond it was almost impossible to get any decay, with the Lowry it was easy. As long as you held down a key on the Hammond, the sound did not die away. On the Lowry the note would fade away quite happily.

The beginning of 'Lucy', that hesitant, lilting introductory phrase, is crucial to the staying power of the song. It is also a marvellous piece of composition, based around five notes only, and so simple that virtually anyone can play it. Schubert would have been proud of it. Nothing in the world is more difficult than to write a first-class melody – especially one that uses as few notes of the scale as we find in 'Lucy'. It is the mark of a great composer: and something that both Lennon and McCartney could do – and did often.

The melody is a falling scale in the left hand, a rocking scale in the right. Curiously, this introductory fragment was not formally composed; it evolved from the chords that John originated for the song, and in a similar way to 'Strawberry Fields Forever', Paul improvised in his favourite arpeggio style until the magic phrase arrived.

The sound we got out of the Lowry reminded me of a BBC radio show I listened to in my teens, featuring a group called Arthur Young and his Novachords. (This must have been back in the 1930s, at the dawn of time!) The eponymous 'Novachord' – an instrument popularized, presumably, by Mr Young – made a lovely

102

sound: crystalline, bell-like: the characteristic sound, in fact, we wanted and eventually got for this track.

A very simple song, then, using that opening phrase as a root for the voice on top.

John, as he often did, composed the song on the hoof: he had the introduction written, but little else as far as the melody went, until we actually got into the studio. Then he came up with that amazing, resonant line: 'Picture yourself in a boat on the river . . .' He sang it almost on one single note, as a monotone over the top of the backing. It was only as we went on with the various takes that he saw the advantages of being a bit more elaborate with the vocal line.

It could have been a monotonous verse, but instead the effect of that almost-single-note vocal against the inspired introductory notes is mesmeric, compelling.

'Lucy In The Sky With Diamonds' is also like 'A Day In The Life', in that it is virtually two separate songs. The middle section is in a completely different tempo and has a completely different time signature to the opening. John has us jump, quite suddenly, from the opening 3/4 into a big 4/4 rhythm.

There was no possibility of making a smooth transition at this point in the song. The big change of tempo had to kick in with a great big bang, a bit like making a clutchless gear change in a car: it crunches, but it keeps you moving forward. The blaring worked, and was the most effective way of doing the song.

The lyrics to 'Lucy' were unlike anything we had heard before in popular music, even 'Strawberry Fields Forever'. Ethereal, dream-like, they were brimming over with the strongest imagery and colour. Combined with the other-worldly music, the surreal Jabberwocky words took you straight into a universe of hallucinogenic fantasy – without having to take any artificial stimulant beforehand!

Paul has told me of the genesis of this marvellous song:

I went out to Weybridge one afternoon as usual to John's house and the first thing he showed me on arrival was a picture that his son Julian had drawn at school. This consisted of a young girl floating in the air with a couple of childishly drawn stars beside her.

103

Across the top of the paper in very neat schoolboy writing in pencil were the words 'Lucy in the Sky with Diamonds'. John explained that Julian had a friend at school called Lucy, and this was her portrait. He said to me that he thought this would be a great title for a song and I agreed. We then went up to the music room at the top of the house and he played me the idea he had for it, starting with *'Picture yourself...'* We discussed Lewis Carroll and the Alice books and how this title would make a great psychedelic song. We began to trade images with each other. I suggested *'cellophane flowers'* – cellophane having been a favourite word of mine since childhood – and then shortly after that I came up with *'newspaper taxis'*. John liked both and countered with *'the girl with kaleidoscope eyes'*. As everyone knows, the song was generally believed to be a deliberate use of the initials LSD in the title, but this was only something we discovered later, and certainly was not intended. Nevertheless, the lyrics were intentionally psychedelic.

When John first sang this track, not only did he sing it in a monotone, he also separated each syllable very distinctly and deliberately: 'Ce – llo – phane – flo – wers – of – ye – llo – and – green . . .' Paul says on the master tape, 'That sounds a bit funny, John. Can we make it smoother?' 'OK,' came the nonchalant reply.

Apart from George Harrison's guitar work on the Beatles recordings, and the wonderful songs he wrote for them, his main influence was in coming up with ideas for sounds, particularly sounds that would create or contribute to the mood of a song. The tamboura drone that gives 'Lucy In The Sky With Diamonds' much of its languorous weight would never have been on the track without George. Similarly the swordmandel on 'Strawberry Fields Forever' was his idea, and again it works brilliantly in terms of fixing a certain atmosphere for the song.

I had to be able to add to the recording the next day (or, as usual, night!), and there was still an awful lot to get done. So I decided to lump all the evening's work on to one track, which meant that Track 1 of the new tape contained nothing less than George's acoustic guitar – now treated with 'wow' – Paul's Lowry organ, George's overdubbed tamboura drone, and Ringo's drums. Quite a handful!

We started again on 2 March with both Paul and Ringo playing overdubs. Paul was on the bass as usual. When George added his electric guitar, we recorded his amp through the Leslie loudspeaker – the rotating speaker from the Hammond organ – which gave us a nice swirly sound.

My frugality with the tracks was paying off . . . I still had two tracks left for the vocals.

The vocals on 'Lucy' weren't recorded at normal speed. The first was recorded at a frequency of forty-five cycles, our normal recording frequency being fifty cycles. In other words, we slowed the tape down, so that when we played it back the voice sounded ten per cent higher: back in the correct key, but thinner-sounding, which suited the song. It gave a slightly Mickey Mouse quality to the vocals. In fact, Paul was also singing on these two tracks, lending John a spot of harmony. I also added the odd bit of tape echo to the voices. The second voice track we recorded at forty-eight-and-a-half cycles per second, to see what that sounded like. 'Lucy' has more variations of tape speed in it than any other track on the album.

On top of all those takes that night we also made eleven mono mixes, all of which, including the eleventh mix marked 'best', we wiped the following day. They just weren't good enough. The day after that, Friday, we worked on the horns to 'Sgt. Pepper's Lonely Hearts Club Band', the opening track, but also recorded four fresh mono mixes of 'Lucy', one of which emerged as best.

All the mixes I did with the Beatles were mono. When I came to do the stereo mixes, there were no Beatles present. In 1967, very few people had stereo equipment. Almost everyone listened on mono; it was accepted as the standard. Stereo was strictly for the hi-fi freaks!

'Lucy', which had no strings, horns or any other classical instruments on it whatsoever, was one of the quickest recordings we did on *Pepper*.

A girl with kaleidoscope eyes, marmalade skies, cellophane flowers – these were definitely not conventional adjectives, even for John and Paul; but they were very Salvador Dali: bold, inventive

105

and surreal. Rocking-horse people eating marshmallow pies, though – that was John more in his Jabberwocky mood. Dali, Dylan Thomas and Lewis Carroll – that was John.

CHAPTER THIRTEEN

9 March 1967:
'A little better all the time . . .'

In his 1968 official biography of the Beatles, Hunter Davies recounts how Paul had the idea for 'Getting Better' while he, Paul and Paul's sheepdog, Martha, were walking together on London's Primrose Hill. Paul had remarked, 'It's getting better!' meaning that the weather was improving and that spring was in the air.

Then he remembered Jimmy Nicol, a replacement drummer the Beatles had for live performances when Ringo was ill with tonsillitis in June 1964. Jimmy always answered, 'Oh, it's getting better all the time,' when they asked him how things were going. As soon as he got home, Paul picked up his guitar and started work on the song.

On Thursday 9 March our usual engineers Geoff Emerick and Richard Lush had a night off, to give them a bit of a break. Malcolm Addy was brought in, along with Ken Townsend. (Malcolm Addy had worked with Norrie Paramor on all the Cliff Richard recordings – but we weren't going to hold that against him!)

Malcolm remembers that the session was arranged for the normal 7 p.m. start time. Nobody turned up – in fact there were very few Beatles to be seen before midnight. Ringo strolled in some time after eleven, and immediately ordered fish and chips. The others turned up later still.

They were beginning to take the people at Abbey Road a bit for granted. Maybe Paul had been polishing up his song – but he wasn't even the last to arrive. Work didn't get under way until about one in the morning – after John had arrived. I didn't ask where he'd been.

We spent two nights laying down the basic rhythm track, a very stringy sound with a relentless driving rhythm. I played a pianette, an early kind of electric piano, which gave us a funny kind of plucking sound, a cross between a harpsichord and a Fender Rhodes electric piano. The modern equivalent would be the cheapest Casio electric keyboard, only the Casio is about twenty times more sophisticated than the pianette. I made noises hitting the strings of this thing, rather than the keys, looking for ways to vary the sound. (Electronic instruments were still extremely primitive in 1967. Robert Moog was working on upgrading the first commercially available synthesizer around the time we were making *Pepper* – only we didn't know about it.)

There is a particular point in 'Getting Better' (it occurs before the line 'Me used to be angry young man . . .') where we all hit a bottom note, a suspended heavy pedal note, which is made up of guitars, tamboura and me thumping the strings of the pianette. This gave us a drone effect that worked really well against the excellent falsetto backing vocals that were now a strong characteristic of the Beatles' sound.

The bones of the taping were:

TRACK 1: bass guitar – Paul
      drums – Ringo
TRACK 2: pianette – George Martin
TRACK 3: more drums – Ringo (overdubbed later)
TRACK 4: guide vocal – Paul

The next day, 10 March, we judged Take 7 best.

After two nights of not very productive work I transferred our first, four-track tape to a second, creating a new basic master. This had most of the backing on Track 1, but I kept the drums and bass guitar separate on Track 2. Meanwhile, on Track 3 we added piano and the tamboura. I played the piano – with a mallet. Not great fun for the piano, maybe – getting bashed right in the vitals – but a great sound, which was just right.

Eleven days later, on 21 March, we took the highly unusual step of dubbing down again, to a third four-track tape. Geoff Emerick was back in the engineer's seat, and we completed the song by putting rhythm and tamboura on Track 1, bass and piano on Track 2, and vocals on the remaining two tracks. Ringo didn't come to the studio that night.

During the time of the Beatles' recordings, Abbey Road studios was a fort in a state of perpetual siege. Even in the middle of the night, fans surged and pressed up relentlessly against the gates. Occasionally it would be impossible to get through them. Somehow or other the adoring multitude had a very efficient grapevine going. They always knew when we were about to arrive, and they all went home once we had left for the night. (Touchingly, many of the girls would have flasks of coffee and sandwiches ready in case the Beatles were in need of refreshment after their labours.) Everybody who worked there just had to get used to the place being like Mafeking before the siege was lifted. This meant that when John became ill that night, there was nowhere I could take him for a breather – except upwards.

I was standing next to John, discussing some finer point of the arrangement to 'Getting Better' when he suddenly looked up at me. 'George,' he said slowly, 'I'm not feeling too good. I'm not focusing on me.'

This was a pretty odd thing to say, even for John. I studied him. I'd been oblivious to it until then, but he did look pretty awful – not sick, but twitchy and strange. 'Do you want someone to take you home?' I asked.

'No,' he replied, 'I don't want to go home.'

'Come on, John,' I said. 'What you need is a breath of fresh air. I know the way up on to the roof.' When we had clambered out on to the flat roof of Studio No. 2, we found it was a beautiful clear night. John took a deep breath, and, with a bit of a lurch, took a couple of steps towards the edge of the building. I grabbed hold of his arm: it was a good fifty feet to the ground. We stood there for a minute or two, with John swaying gently against my arm. 'I'm feeling better,' he announced. Then he looked up at the stars. 'Wow . . .' he intoned. 'Look at that! Isn't that amazing?'

I followed his gaze. The stars did look good, and there seemed to be a great many of them – but they didn't look that good. It was very unlike John to be over the top in that way. I stared at him. He was wired – pin-sharp and quivering, resonating away like a human tuning-fork.

No sooner had John uttered his immortal words about the stars than George and Paul came bursting out on to the roof. They had come tearing up from the studio as soon as they found out where we were.

They knew why John was feeling unwell. Maybe everyone else did, too – everyone except for father-figure George Martin here!

It was very simple. John was tripping on LSD. He had taken it by mistake, they said – he had meant to take an amphetamine tablet. That hardly made any difference, frankly; the fact was that John was only too likely to imagine he could fly, and launch himself off the low parapet that ran around the roof. They had been absolutely terrified that he might do so.

> **We took several substances, but not when we were actually playing, because we found out very early on that if you play it stoned or derelict in any way it was really shitty music, so we would have the experiences and then bring that into the music later.**
>
> – Ringo, *South Bank Show*

I spoke to Paul about this night many years later, and he confirmed that he and George had been shaken rigid when they found out we were up on the roof. They knew John was having what you might call a bad trip. John didn't go back to Weybridge that night; Paul took him home to his place, in nearby Cavendish Road. They were intensely close, remember, and Paul would do almost anything for John. So, once they were safely inside, Paul took a tablet of LSD for the first time, 'So I could get with John,' as he put it – be with him in his misery and fear.

What about that for friendship?

> **I never took it in the studio. Once I did, actually. I thought I was taking some uppers, and I was not in the state of handling it. And I can't remember what album it was. But I took it and I just noticed ... I suddenly got so scared on the mike, I said, 'What is it? I feel ill ...'**
>
> –*John Lennon Remembers*

This occasion was the first, and the last, time I saw John, or any of the Beatles, unable to work in the studio. The Beatles' attitude to Abbey Road meant that they would never have wanted to take anything, anyway. They worked, we all worked, incredibly hard, in terms of the hours we put in, the intensity of the creative effort. To them, though, the studio was a giant workshop. They enjoyed being there. It wasn't so much work, in the strict sense of the word, as 'Let's make some music. Ring up George and tell him we want to be round there at eight o'clock.' The Beatles, during *Pepper*, were happy with what they were doing. Drugs and alcohol tend to be abused when people dislike the reality they are living through. Sorry, but it's the truth.

Once, when I was feeling a bit down, John popped something into my hand. 'Here you are, George,' he said. 'This'll do you wonders.' I looked down, and there was a little capsule in my hand, of the kind you might take for a cold or the flu. I kept it, and showed it to Norman Cowan, my doctor. 'What is this, Norman?' I asked. He stared down at it, aghast. 'My God,' he said in a panicky sort of way, 'where did you get that? Don't you dare take it. In fact, give it to me, now . . .!'

To this day I don't know what it was. Maybe I missed something.

That wasn't the end of 'Getting Better'. Two days later, on 23 March, the Beatles were back in the studio overdubbing vocals and Ringo's bongo drums. There was another tape-to-tape reduction – but without me. The song was there, but they were just polishing it up.

> **. . . one of the great things was that the music papers started to slag us off, because we hadn't done anything, because it took five months to record, and I remember the great glee seeing in one of the papers how the Beatles have dried up, there's nothing coming from them, they're stuck in the studio, they can't think what they're doing, and I was sitting rubbing my hands, saying 'You just wait.'** – Paul, *South Bank Show*

Whenever Paul was at his honey-sugar-candy mostest, John would be there with his test-tube at the ready. Plink! In would go just that little twist of Lennon, bringing the song up sharply and steering it away from the commonplace and the predictable. 'Getting Better' is a good case in point: it was John who added the line 'It couldn't get much worse,' as a counterbalance to the super-optimism of the first verse.

111

This is how it happened: Paul, George and Ringo arrived at the studio well before John. Paul had been running through the song on the old upright piano in No. 2 studio so we could all learn it. He had got to the part where it starts again, and was singing, 'I've got to admit it's getting better, A little better all the time,' when John strode through the doors at the far end of the studio. Instantly, and having never heard a note of the song before in his life, he started singing the perfect musical and lyrical counter: 'It can't get much worse.' And his line gave the song just that little edge it needed.

CHAPTER FOURTEEN

The Album Cover

I would go in on a Saturday morning, to a place in Liverpool called Lewis's, with me ten bob, buy my record, and then sit on the bus for half-an-hour afterwards, and read the cover. I'd take it out of the bag, read it, read the label, read anything I could get my eyes on. So on *Pepper* I thought, This is it, it's an overall concept, we'll have the cover packed with little things, so three months from now you'll go, 'Oh, I never saw that . . .' The whole idea was to put everything, the whole world into this package; that's why we got Peter Blake in . . .

— Paul, *South Bank Show*

Around this point, we started working on the album cover. The *Sgt. Pepper* cover, like the music inside it, was intended to blow people's minds, and it did. It was like a shaft of sunlight penetrating an old mine. It caught the zesty excitability, the rainbow confidence and colour of the day. It also caught on. It sparked a massive cult following, a kind of cover-cult that grew and grew until it was a wholesale industry in its own right. This was especially true in our biggest market, the United States.

There were quizzes nationwide to see who could name all the faces in the photograph. Peter Blake was probably the only person alive then who could do this, and even he would have had a hard time putting a name to all of George's Indian gurus. The *Sunday Times* newspaper stole a march on its rivals by publishing a key to the faces, but even that was not complete. Despite all the attempts

113

at demystification, though, myths about the cover still sprang up, fully formed, from thin air.

Until *Sgt. Pepper*, album covers had been rather boring, almost without exception. It used to make me very angry, the way the record companies would present good products so badly. To my way of thinking, the cover was as significant as what it contained. Obviously, it was the thing that people first saw when they went out to buy, the thing on which many people based their first impressions.

Paul was very much into art at this time, going to galleries and beginning to collect paintings. Robert Fraser, the West End gallery owner, was a friend of his, advising him on what he might like to buy. Beatles' protégés Simon Posthuma and Marijke Koger, the Dutch design team who called themselves 'The Fool', had already designed an other-worldly cover for the album. Fraser wasn't sure about it. He showed this cover to a couple of artists he represented, Peter Blake and Jann Haworth, and asked them, 'What do you think of this? It's very psychedelic, isn't it? Do you think something more could be done with it?' Both artists looked at the Fool's effort and replied that they thought something could.

Fraser suggested to the Beatles that they commission Blake and Haworth to design an alternative. This was a very smart move, since Peter was, and is, one of the founder members of the Pop Art movement, which began in Britain and America back in the late fifties, with people like Richard Hamilton, Jasper Johns, and of course Peter himself. Blake was well known for, among other things, his highly innovative use of collage.

Even better, Blake's wife and artistic partner, Jann Haworth, agreed to help him out on the assignment. Jann was an established artist in her own right, a founder-member with Blake of the Ruralist school of painting. She had already exhibited 'tableaux' as she called them – groups of cloth figures and animals – at the 'Young Contemporaries' show at the ICA in 1963. Some of these figures, like the 'Old Lady', and 'Shirley Temple', were to find posterity on the *Sgt. Pepper* cover.

Once they had agreed to come on board, Paul McCartney invited Peter and Jann round to his house, where he played them a few of the *Sgt. Pepper* tracks on a tape, to give them the general idea of what the album would be like. Peter and Paul already knew each other, anyway, because Paul had commissioned Blake to do a painting for him two years before, in 1965. Peter had come up with an exact copy of Landseer's *The Monarch of the Glen*, but with a Pop Art caption on it saying what it was.

You might have expected Peter, being an artist, to want to paint something for the *Pepper* cover, but he didn't. When he came on board, the Beatles had already had the 'Northern brass band' uniforms made, a fair bit of the recording was complete, and the loose *Sgt. Pepper* concept was in place. What Peter picked up on was the idea of the Beatles stepping outside themselves. That is why he arranged to borrow the waxwork figures of the Beatles from Madame Tussaud's, the idea being that if the people in the brightly coloured uniforms were Sgt Pepper's Lonely Hearts Club Band, then why couldn't the Beatles be other people entirely, looking on?

Paul's original thought was to have the Beatles in a park being given a formal presentation by the Lord Mayor or some such character. They were to be situated behind a huge floral clock, such as exist in many Northern parks. There could be a wonderful magic crowd in this imaginary park – an imaginary audience watching and listening. George, Paul and John gave Peter Blake a list of the characters they wanted, but Jann Haworth, Robert Fraser and Peter Blake made their own lists too, just for the heck of it.

John Lennon put in people like Aleister Crowley, the black magician, Adolf Hitler, Jesus, Albert Stubbins, the Liverpool footballer (John did not know who Stubbins was, really; he just knew his dad liked him). His inclusion of figures like Hitler, who was definitely not a hero of his, was just to be a naughty boy. John knew full well that these figures would not be used, especially after the furore over his remarks about Christianity. He just thought he'd try it on, for a joke – even including Jesus Christ on his list to see what would happen! Hitler does appear in some of the original photographic transparencies, but he was eventually removed.

Peter Blake's list included Dion, of Dion and the Belmonts, Leo Gorcey and Huntz Hall of the Bowery Boys, Richard Lindner and Richard Merkin, both painters. Rober Fraser put in lots of West Coast painters, people who had exhibited at his gallery. George, of course, wanted twelve Indian gurus. Ringo just said, 'You carry on, fine,' and never made a list. They didn't ask me for my heroes; otherwise we might have had J. S. Bach and R. J. Mitchell (the designer of the Spitfire) in the tableau as well. Curiously, none of the characters from the songs, like Mr Kite or Lovely Rita, made an appearance. Peter and Jann pasted the photographs, blown-up to life-size, of all these people on to pieces of hardboard.

Along with the *Pepper* tableau's cloth figures, Jann Haworth came up with a number of other original ideas for the venture. Passing the municipal flower-clock in Hammersmith, West London, one day in the car with Paul (it is still there today, under the A40 flyover), she said that it would be very nice not to have real lettering on the *Sgt. Pepper* cover but do something like that kind of civic flower-bed lettering. The letters and words, she suggested, would in this way become an integral part of the whole 'band in the park' idea.

Blake and Haworth created what is really a form of sculpture, with cut-outs, plants, props and wax figures. Their artwork on the sleeve complements the music inside it perfectly: both are types of collage. Jann spent a long time building a background, a scene against which the Beatles would be photographed, hanging the first row of photographs on the studio wall, then fixing the other blow-ups on poles and spacing them in tiers at intervals of a foot or so, to give the picture the illusion of depth.

Haworth also did all the hand-tinting of the original black-and-white photographs.

It was Peter who put in the waxworks of Sonny Liston and Diana Dors. He was having great fun doing his own thing, at the same time as doing the Beatles' bidding. He now wishes he'd put more musicians in the picture, especially Chuck Berry.

The Beatles paid Robert Fraser £1500 to put the package together. He in turn sub-contracted the work to Blake and Haworth, paying them just £200 between them.

Blake asked Joe Ephgrave, a fairground artist, to paint a couple of drum skins in a suitably imaginative and circusy style. Ephgrave, unaided, did a brilliant job, inspiring many imitations. (The drum skin painting used on the cover ended up in John Lennon's New York home; the other skin is in a private collection.)

There is a bust of T. E. Lawrence, in the midst of the famous 'marijuana plants'. These plants, the small green ones just in front of the drum and again on the right at the very bottom of the front cover photograph, caused a lot of controversy in their day. The

ANYONE AT HOME?
Outside Brian's house in Chapel Street

WE MADE IT INSIDE!

LINDA SHOOTS PAUL, 1967

GETTING BETTER ALL THE TIME
The two Georges with Paul

NO ONE I THINK IS IN MY TREE **EXCEPT PERHAPS ME**
John and Paul in the 'Strawberry Fields' video

ALL YOU NEED IS LOVE
(and a touch of genius)

JUST IN CASE YOU DON'T UNDERSTAND PLAIN ENGLISH
The multinational live broadcast of 'All You Need Is Love'

WHERE'S THE ORCHESTRA?
A run-through of 'All You Need Is Love'

GEORGE WITH HIS MENTOR, RAVI SHANKAR

A BIT OF HULA *An early video after the release of* Sgt. Pepper

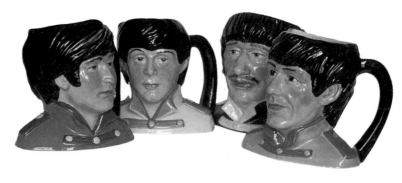

MUG SHOTS

INFLATED BEATLES
Some of the Sgt. Pepper *merchandise*

FAN FARE   Sgt. Pepper *keyrings and badges*

A COLOURFUL RECORD
A specially printed limited vinyl edition

spiky little green villains were widely accused of being cannabis plants. In fact they are a very well-kept secret joke. Their real Latin name is – *Peperomia* . . .! The funny thing is, nobody can remember who played this joke.

The rest of the foliage is easily identifiable, as nothing more sinister than hyacinths, maidenhair fern, Kentia palms and azaleas, but I don't think any of these conceal any further puns or witticisms!

The foliage must be botanically correct, anyway, because it came from one of London's most prestigious and long-established garden centres, Clifton Nurseries, in Maida Vale, London. It is unlikely that they would be in the business of supplying the dreaded weed! The nursery is still there thriving to this day.

The youngest of the three boys who delivered the plants (not nearly as many as were requested, in the event) was a big Beatles fan. He asked if he could contribute something to the cover, and made the guitar in the foreground of the photograph out of yellow hyacinths, with green planting canes laid over it for strings. The flowers that make up this guitar can be read as 'Paul?' – according to the seekers after proof of Paul's 'death'. They must have squinted hard and employed a very large amount of imagination.

. . . We were trying to say we like these people, they are part of our life . . . – George Harrison, *South Bank Show*

There are no fewer than three images of Shirley Temple: the Jann Haworth cloth doll wearing the 'Welcome Rolling Stones' shirt (which belonged to Adam Cooper, the photographer's son); the standing image of Shirley just to the right of Marlene Dietrich, sheltering under the curvaceous arm and low-cut golden dress of Diana Dors; and another photograph of the infant star, peeping up between John and Ringo's waxwork likenesses, on the left-hand side of the cover (her face is partly obscured by them). So Shirley Temple definitely comes out at the top of the collective cover popularity poll. Either that, or she figured on three separate lists and nobody noticed that she had slipped into the limelight three times!

The Beatles wanted all these images, but they had not thought about the potential copyright problems. I knew there was going to be trouble. Years before *Pepper* I had chosen the cover of an album I had produced by a Scots recording artist called Jimmy Shand. I got hold of a lovely photo of a guy in a kilt staring soulfully across a majestic highland scene. Irresistible, thought I, to far-flung Scots everywhere, who would flock in their thousands to buy this idealized picture of their homeland. (They didn't.) The picture came from an agency. Alas! After the record was issued, EMI was threatened with a law suit by a certain Scottish Member of Parliament. He said we were using his image to promote the record without his permission, and he wanted damages, or a fee. Naturally I had had no idea that the photograph was of a real person (and not an actor, who would clearly be unreal!) and an MP at that. The case was settled out of court, and I was rapped firmly over the knuckles.

Against this sort of background, it was not very surprising that Sir Joseph Lockwood, head of EMI, took one look at the proposed *Pepper* cover and said, 'This is nonsense; we're not having this.'

'We will have it,' replied the Beatles, who by this time were quite aware of their vast power and importance to the company. A major battle ensued. In the end, Joe said to Brian Epstein, who always got lumbered with this sort of problem, 'OK, if you want to do it, you've got to get all the clearances. EMI is not going to be responsible. And whatever happens, some of those faces have got to go: I'm not having Gandhi, for a start, there's enough trouble in India without stirring up more. And Hitler is a definite no.'

'All right,' shot back Paul, when he heard about Sir Joe's strictures, 'I'll trade him two Marlon Brandos for a Gandhi!'

Brian trudged off back to his office, worrying about yet another hurdle. As always, like many a man who has his back to the wall, he turned to his resourceful p.a.: Wendy Hanson. There was only one small snag: Wendy no longer worked for him . . .

Brian had flown into one irrational pill-induced rage too many one day, and Wendy had walked out on him for good at the end of 1966. Now the Beatles trusted very, very few people: they had been let down too many times; but they knew they could always trust Wendy. Brian trusted her absolutely. They also knew that if anyone could achieve the impossible it was she.

Brian called her up.

'Now Wendy,' he began, 'there's a leetle, tiny problem I have here ...' He explained the nature of the task, the difficulty and complexity of which would have made Hercules think several times before taking it on. Predictably, Wendy demurred. Brian tried wheedling. Wendy still wasn't having any of it. So he resorted to a bit of the old soft soap: 'It's really for the boys, darling. You know how they trust you. And Sir Joe adores you. Be a darling—'

'Oh, don't be ridiculous, Brian,' snapped back Wendy, who was nobody's fool. 'All right, I'll do it; but on one condition: that I can pick your legal brains whenever I need to. That way I will learn everything there is to know about copyright and photographers, which I need just now.'

'Done,' said Brian. And, eventually, it was.

Wendy Hanson's new job, working for film producer David Puttnam, was as a photographer's agent, a field about which she knew very little. The *Pepper* cover would be the ideal way of finding out, fast; or so she thought.

In fact, as she said later, the whole thing was a nightmare, from start to finish. First she had to find out who each person featured on the cover was – in itself far from easy; then she had to write to them individually asking their permission for the shot to be included. Next job was to find out who had taken the original photograph, and obtain written permission from them for its use. There were more than sixty people to contact, not including the photographers. She spent her days putting in transatlantic calls to Fred Astaire, to Johnny Weissmuller, Marlon Brando, and a host of others, and waiting anxiously for them to call back.

Most of the heroes agreed without any problems; but not all. Leo Gorcey, one of the Dead End Kids, who was one of John's choices, demanded five hundred dollars for the privilege of using his mug-shot, so he came out straight away! Gorcey was originally placed between the actor Huntz Hall and the 'Varga girl' in the back row; you can still just make out a vague outline where his face once used to be. His features were taken out at the photographic stage of the printing. (This was a kinder, artistic version of the old Soviet Communist Party habit of 'unpersoning' party leaders who had fallen from grace – by simply airbrushing their faces out of all official photographs, with a stunning contempt for historical accuracy!)

Another slight hiccup occurred in the case of Mae West. After Wendy had contacted Mae asking for her consent, the ballsy star sent back a note which read, 'What would I be doing in a Lonely Hearts Club? You can't leave me in.' And of course she had a point. What would the great siren of stage and screen be doing in a club for the emotionally unfulfilled? Everybody wanted her in, though: after all, anyone who had spent ten days in prison for obscenity and given her name to a life-jacket had to be a heroine. Wendy got the Beatles to write a reply, which they all signed, expressing their unanimous admiration for Mae.

Mae capitulated.

Poor Wendy; once she'd finally completed the Herculean job on the cover clearances, she had great difficulty in getting Brian to pay her for it. The fee he had promised was only fifty pounds, so it wasn't meanness that stopped him paying her; it was absent-mindedness.

He eventually settled up by sending the money round in cash. To add insult to injury, however, an interview with Peter Brown, Brian's new assistant, who replaced Wendy, appeared in the *Daily Express* a little while afterwards. The article quoted Brown as saying how difficult it had been for him to sort out the cover! Wendy wrote Brian a furious note.

'You know what journalists are like, Wendy,' replied Brian lamely. 'I'm sure Peter didn't say that. They're always making up quotes . . .'

As to the Beatles' own image on the album cover, the satin uniforms they had made for the photograph were of course completely over the top, but that was what they liked about them. They fancied that image of themselves. It sent up the military (that is, the US military in Vietnam), which was very politically correct at the time. They had the outfits specially made for them by Berman's, the London theatrical outfitters.

John brought in the small portable television for the cover shot. 'Television,' he assured us, 'is very important to me just now.'

The photographer who took the famous shot was a friend of Robert Fraser's, Michael Cooper. Michael, a great cameraman who took hundreds of shots of the Rolling Stones, died tragically a few years after *Pepper* came out.

There's a wonderful spirit in them which captures the time without being self-conscious. They are very intimate. – Jann Haworth on Michael Cooper's photographs
of the period in his anthology, *Blinds and Shutters*

The art of the vinyl album sleeve, if you accept that it is art, did not have much of a life before the Beatles. Now, in 1993, with the arrival of the compact disc, it is already dead and buried. There was a retrospective exhibition of the album cover genre recently, with prices for the original artwork commanding increasingly large figures: which proves that cover-art must be art – and that it must be dead!

We were a long way from the sparseness of the first Beatles album cover, 'Please Please Me', which was done in an almighty rush, like the music. I said, 'Come on, let's do this looking-upwards shot here.' We rang up the legendary theatre photographer Angus McBain, and bingo, he came round and did it there and then, on the balcony of EMI House. Thereafter, though, the Beatles' own creativity came bursting to the fore.

I suddenly realized with all those Sergeant Pepper moustaches where all that came from. I had an accident on a moped and bust my lip ... and being always in photo sessions, we always had to do that, it was very embarrassing to have this big fat lip, so I started to grow this moustache to hide it, and then the others sort of said, 'Hey, that's good,' and so without anyone knowing we all just grew these moustaches ... it wasn't a 'look' at all, it was just a kid growing a moustache for a laugh ...
– Paul, *South Bank Show*

This shaggy rash is spreading over the face of Britain. On the face of it, you're nobody in England these days if you haven't got half an inch of nicotine-stained hair hanging from your stiff upper lip ... There's Sean Connery, Terence Stamp, Brian Epstein,

Pete Townshend, Keith Richards ... Maybe you're wondering why this ugly rash has suddenly spread across the face of Britain ... The easy and correct answer is that drooping Mexican-style moustaches have suddenly become 'in'. They're in because George Harrison grew one while learning to play the sitar in India ... and as if that were not enough all the Beatles have now grown moustaches. When I heard that I just had to have one too.

– Christopher Ward, *Daily Mirror*

15 March 1967: 'With our love—we could save the world . . .'

Maharishi's Academy of Transcendental Meditation is situated on a big flat ledge, like a giant-sized shelf, 150 feet above the River Ganges. The views from this Ashram (that's the name given by the Indians to any holy place, anywhere where people come to study and meditate) are wonderful. You look out over the river, across to the town of Rishikesh and the plains beyond. There are mountains on the other three sides and jungle all about. Colourful peacocks strut about; you see a monkey or two at every glance, staring down at you from almost every branch of the trees. — Mal Evans, *The Beatles Monthly Book*, May 1968

George Harrison was what you might call the Beatles' Third Man — always there, yet somehow elusive. Paul had introduced him to John when they were all teenage schoolboys learning chords on their guitars. Unfortunately for him, George was a few, crucially spotty years younger than John. Perhaps because of this age difference, John was condescending towards George in those early days, and this was still apparent when I first met them all. Later on, this uneasiness seemed to evaporate as the business of being a professional Beatle took over. Some undercurrent between the two men may yet have remained to the very end, though: the only people who came to actual blows with one another on 'Let It Be' were John and George.

The electricity that crackled between Paul and John, and that led to such great music, rather left George out in the cold. He had only himself to collaborate with. If he needed help from the other two, they gave it, but often rather grudgingly. It was not so much that Lennon and McCartney did not believe in Harrison; more that their overwhelming belief in themselves left very little room for anything – or anybody – else.

As for my own role, I am sorry to say that I did not help George much with his song writing, either. His early attempts didn't show enormous promise. Being a very pragmatic person, therefore, I tended to go with the blokes who were delivering the goods. I never cold-shouldered George. I did, though, look at his new material with a slightly jaundiced eye.

When he brought a new song along to me, even before he had played it, I would say to myself, 'I wonder if it is going to be any better than the last one?' It was in this light that I looked at the first number he brought me for the *Sgt. Pepper* album, which was 'It's Only A Northern Song'. I groaned inside when I heard it. We did make a recording of it on 14 February, but I knew it was never going to make it.

I had to tell George that as far as *Pepper* was concerned, I did not think his song would be good enough for what was shaping up as a really strong album. I suggested he come up with something a bit better. George was a bit bruised: it is never pleasant being rejected, even if you are friendly with the person who is doing the rejecting. ('It's Only A Northern Song' did see the light of day in the end, on *Yellow Submarine*.)

When he came up with 'Within You Without You', then, as a replacement, it was a bit of a relief all round. He'd composed it after an intense late-night conversation with his mate Klaus Voormann about the meaning of life. This song was really different; and although George had experimented with Indian music quite a bit before *Sgt. Pepper* – the sitar in 'Norwegian Wood' springs to mind – this was the first time he'd devoted an entire track to his obsession.

'Within You Without You' demanded Indian musicians. It was nothing whatsoever like anything John or Paul could have come up with, and in that lay much of its appeal for me. I still didn't think of it as a great song, though (many now do!). The tune struck me as being a little bit of a dirge; but I found what George wanted to do with the song fascinating. It was cosmically different – weird! The lyrics touched on what you might call the metaphysical: the inner meaning of life, and all that kind of thing. And it was deeply anti-establishment.

'Within You Without You', like Paul's 'She's Leaving Home' and 'Yesterday', was a distinctly solo effort. Looking back, these one-offs were early signs of the group's disintegration. The Beatles had been prisoners of their 'Fab Four' straitjacket for about five years – a very long time in pop music, even then. Look at today's charts and see how many people last as long as five years. Five months, in some cases, if that.

When he first played it to me on his acoustic guitar, George made rather a mournful sound: but I was intrigued. He had a host of Indian musicians who were friends of his, some of whom he called in to play a guide rhythm track with him. George loved working with these musicians, and it was fascinating to see how his ideas grew, and how easily he communicated the complex music to them. Indian rhythms can be extraordinarily difficult, and I have a fond memory of George speaking in a strange tongue, emphasizing the accents with a wag of his head – 'Ta-ta ticky ta, ticky tick ta ta' and so on. The Indian musicians cottoned on instantly. It was most impressive. I, too, knew a few of the musicians from the Asian Music Circle in London, because of my previous work with Peter Sellers.

After producing 'Goodness Gracious Me', Peter's big 1960 cod-Indian hit, I'd had the idea to repeat the formula with the song, 'Wouldn't It Be Lovely?' from *My Fair Lady*. Peter thought this was a great hoot. 'We'll give it an authentic Indian backing . . .' I said. I contacted the Asian Music Circle, who provided us with sitar and tabla players. There was only one small snag: the sitar player spoke no English. When I explained that I wanted her to play along with the rhythm track of the song we had already recorded, she would start playing as I was speaking. When I called down from the control room for her to play, she would stop. We got it right eventually, but it took a while. I learned a great deal about the sitar, and about Indian music in the process!

But the dilruba player for 'Within You Without You' I had not met, nor had I come across the bowed instrument he was playing. It is a kind of one-string fiddle, which makes characteristic slurps and swooping sounds: to me, it was a completely closed book. 'This one is going to be meaty,' I thought to myself.

There is pop music in India, of course, as there is anywhere else; it tends to be film sound-track music. There is also a rich tradition of folk music in the sub-continent, and north and south Indian classical music, each with its own further subdivisions. George had looked into all this pretty thoroughly, and had homed in on Hindustani north Indian classical music as the thing that appealed to him most. This was one of the most ancient forms of music in the world, he told me, mentioned in India's ancient Vedic literature.

What really appealed to George was the sound – the unique sound the instruments made when used in this very ancient tradition. In some mystical way, he told me, he recognized that sound; it was as if he had heard it before.

George understood that in any song written according to the rules of the Vedic tradition the voice and the dilruba should accompany one another in unison. This was true even of what was basically a Western pop tune. It was the instrumentation, not the melody, that made it sound Indian.

So George and I had a difficult task ahead. My job was to add Western strings to the song – that is, to find classically trained European fiddle players (frequently of Jewish stock) and get them to mimic their Indian counterparts. This intrigued me no end. I couldn't wait to see the titanic clash of cultures in the studio! When it came to it, the European string players mingled pretty well with the Indian players, but musically the Europeans were sliding around all over the place. This was especially true in the second, or middle section of 'Within You Without You', where the tabla changes rhythm from a 4/4 to a much more Indian-feeling 5/4 tempo; here, too, the song gets quite fast and tricky. We had a lot of fun getting that right.

We started working on this strange song (which was, incidentally, one of Geoff Emerick's favourites; he loved George's music) on 15 March. It was a long one, at just over five minutes, and it was split into three main parts. Right from the first note, it brims over with Indian instruments: the dilruba, the tamboura drone, the tabla, and the swordmandel – the zither-like plucked instrument we had already used on 'Strawberry Fields Forever'.

When I was about twelve or thirteen I was riding on my bike and I heard 'Heartbreak Hotel' coming out

126

of somebody's house. The sound meant something to me: it just touched me in a certain way and made me want to know about it or follow it. Likewise with Indian music. It didn't make any sense to me, but somewhere inside of me it made absolute sense. It made more sense than anything I had ever heard before. — George, *South Bank Show*

When the Indian instrumentalists arrived hot-foot from exotic Finchley they changed the studio scene – bare walls, bare floor, hostile fridge – pretty dramatically. They scattered carpets on the floor, spread hangings, hunkered down, and generally made themselves at home: suddenly we had colour, life and warmth in our normally cold and featureless surroundings.

George, as usual, set joss-sticks smouldering in the corners. He looked a bit like the Lone Ranger, with his Indian friends. Although the other Beatles were there, they stuck around for the fun of it. None of them played or sang a note. In order to get them to play what he wanted, George would simply sing to the Indian musicians, or occasionally pick a few notes on the sitar.

On that very first evening I met Peter Blake. He had come in to the studios to talk to the boys about their ideas for the album cover, which Paul was trying to organize. Peter had never seen a Beatles recording session, and he was amazed. He thought it was a very gentle, very easy way of working. But it was all the music, really: it was George's hypnotic music that induced that strange air of peace.

And so we began recording:

TRACK 1: looking at our recording sheets for 15 March, we started off with a tamboura drone, as you generally have to with any Indian track. Neil Aspinall was ideal for the tamboura drone; he'd got pretty used to stroking this atmospheric instrument – he'd had plenty of practice on *Revolver*. We had several other tambouras going, though, at the same time, to give us depth in the drone.

TRACK 2: tabla, the percussive Indian drum-sound, along with a small amount of swordmandel.

TRACKS 3 and 4: dilruba, carrying the tune.

The song was basically this tune and the accompanying drone – there were no harmonies in it. In Indian classical music the voice is regarded as the primary instrument. All music, according to Vedic thinking, started through the voice – so it followed that all other instruments were made to copy the voice, and not compete with it in any way.

We finished that night at 1.30 a.m., and left the song for exactly one week, until 22 March, while we were occupied with the album cover. Then we dubbed what we had done on to Tracks 1 and 2 of a second four-track tape. The tablas and tambouras we mixed on to one track, the dilrubas on to the other. We added George's vocals, and, when he was not singing, his sitar, on to Track 4. This left Track 3 for my string score, which I still had to write. This 22 March session was another long one, winding up at 2.15 on the morning of 23 March.

We were getting near the end of the album now, but there was still a little way left to go. We came back in on Monday 3 April, at 7 p.m. as usual, to finish off. 'We', in this case, meant George, myself, and the outside musicians – there were no other Beatles present that night.

It turned out to be a marathon eleven-and-a-half-hour session. We worked our socks off in the big studio, No. 1, until three in the morning, recording the string score I had written to fit the Indian tracks we had already laid down.

I had eight violinists and three cellists, led again by Erich Gruenberg. They were all first-class players in their own right, and they had to be – they found it very difficult indeed to follow and keep up with the elastic swoops and wiry furrows of the dilruba. It was also pretty tedious for them, having to go over and over the same phrase until George was satisfied with it. By now we had only one track left on the tape, so if we did not get everything right on a given take, we just wiped the entire take.

In short, we had to get it right; but we did a lot of takes before George was pleased with the result. George's meticulousness was worth it, in the end. Gruenberg's gentlemen-players did the business: we had added another dimension to the song.

When George was finally satisfied with what we had achieved it was about 3 a.m., and we all assumed we could go home. The musicians did go, they couldn't wait to go – it was well past their bedtime. To my astonishment, though, George himself wanted to carry on.

Propping our eyelids up with joss-sticks, we moved over to

Studio No. 2, across the road, where we spent a further three-and-a-half hours mixing. I eventually got home at seven or so, in time for breakfast. Judy got a cup of tea in bed that morning.

> **I wouldn't have minded being George, the invisible man, and learning what he learned. Maybe it was hard for him sometimes, because Paul and I are such egomaniacs, but that's the game.**
>
> — *John Lennon Remembers*

Despite all our efforts, it still wasn't quite there. So we were back in again that night, at seven, for further mono and stereo mixing until 12.45 the next morning. We did a lot of technical things, like artificially double-tracking the strings, to give them more body. George wanted to dub some laughter on to the end of the song. He didn't want people to feel he was being over-earnest, boring for Britain about the meaning of life, and we found a bit of tape that had the four Beatles cracking up with laughter at the end of some take or other. This spontaneous hilarity was dropped in at the end of the song, and George was happy.

'Within You Without You' is obviously a long way from your normal Western pop song. It has no harmonic structure, no chords, and it doesn't modulate as Western songs generally do. There is the tamboura drone, which gives you a sense of tonality, and the tabla, which gives you a sense of rhythm; but all there is on top of that is the dilruba and vocal line – the tune itself. All the instruments are playing in unison, including the cellos, which are playing an octave lower than the dilruba. Without the strings, the song would have sounded *too* Indian, if anything.

We did make one concession to Western pop music, which was a tiny bit of counterpoint in the melodic line; if you listen, you will hear another line answering it from time to time, but that was the only one.

> **. . . we've had four years doing what everybody else wanted us to do. Now we're doing what we want to do . . . Everything we've done so far has been rubbish as I see it today. Other people may like what we've done, but we're not kidding ourselves. It doesn't**

mean a thing to what we want to do now.

– George Harrison, *Daily Mirror*, 11 November 1966

The other Beatles liked 'Within You Without You', though they were a bit bemused by it. But then that was George – always coming up with the unexpected. They thought it was well worth putting in because of its eccentricity alone.

George did plough a lonely furrow in his music. 'Within You Without You' is very introspective: a distillation of George's studies of Eastern philosophy and music. Although Eastern culture became big during the late sixties, George was one of the first to look east, and the depth of his interest in Vedic philosophy put him way beyond the reach of the trendy pack barking behind him.

Despite what I've said about the relatively marginal position that George's music had within the group, it would be entirely wrong to think that he himself was excluded from it. George had something stronger than power: he had influence. Witness the fact that all of the boys followed him to India to sit at the feet of the Maharishi. George tried to persuade me to ease my karma, too, but I excused myself on the grounds of extreme old age.

The Beatles were all looking for something. They had achieved great fame and fortune, but that had made them wonder all the harder what it meant. They were looking for a greater faith than the half-baked versions of Eastern religion and culture circulating in the West could give them. They all wanted to experiment, to push at the envelope of their upbringing, beliefs and culture. They wanted to find out what it was all about.

George was able to answer some of the questions they asked, and the Maharishi seemed to answer more. He was able to bring them a measure of inner peace, which was something they had not found before.

Although they became disillusioned with it afterwards, trans-cendental meditation was more than a passing fad for the Beatles. It lasted long enough that even after *Sgt. Pepper*, when the Maharishi was visiting Wales, they all rushed off again to sit at his feet. The scales fell from their eyes when it became clear that the guru was after all very much a human being, with feet of clay, but George still to this day will insist: 'OK, that's fair enough, but it

130

doesn't alter the basic truth,' by which he means the truths he learned from Eastern philosophies all those years ago.

The Vedic system is all about enlightenment, basically, and music is one of the vehicles to gain enlightenment. — George Harrison, *South Bank Show*

George always had a very pragmatic streak. He never let the so-called glamour of show-business seduce him. He always saw through phoney people very quickly. He was the practical one, the one who could mend the amplifier or change the fuse. And he is one of the most generous people I know. If you were a friend of George in need, he would reach into his pocket and give you his last penny. Equally, if it were a matter of principle, he would defend you to the last. If ever I were in trouble, George Harrison is the kind of person I would like to be able to turn to.

I think we just grew through those years together, him as the straight man and us as the loonies; but he was always there for us to interpret our madness – we used to be slightly avant-garde on certain days of the week, and he would be there as the anchor person, to communicate that through the engineers on to the tape. — George Harrison, *South Bank Show*

Pepper is a peculiarly English album, despite the exotic flowering of 'Within You Without You'. I suppose it's a bit chicken-and-egg; it is like saying that Mary Quant dresses are 'English'. Well of course they are – she's English. But there is something characteristic of what was happening in England at that time, something in the air that *Pepper*, like a Quant design, expressed. You couldn't have heard anything like *Pepper* from America.

Why? Maybe it is because in spite of their rebelliousness, in spite of their waywardness, in spite of their genius, it was a very disciplined Beatles sound. It was an organized, relatively controlled sound. This is a difficult concept to pin down, but it is like looking at an American car of the time, and then looking at its English counterpart. The American product could be, was often,

131

overblown, over-sized, gross, even, like a Cadillac – all teeth and fins. English cars, on the other hand, tended to be discreetly lined, elegant: the Rolls-Royce Silver Shadow of the time still looks good today.

Pepper has style because it was restrained. It knew when to stop.

17 March 1967:
'Fun is the one thing that money can't buy . . .'

'She's Leaving Home' is one more example of Paul working away at home, coming up with another beautiful ballad that tells its own little story. (Like 'Getting Better', Paul says the song first came to him as he was walking Martha on Primrose Hill.) John added some telling lines in the chorus – against Paul's sustained . . . 'She is leaving . . .' he was to sing the beautiful contrapuntal lines 'We gave her most of our lives'. But there were to be no other Beatles on it. Paul wanted the backing to be strings alone.

By this time, Paul had developed quite a taste for orchestras and classical twirly bits generally, which may be why even he does not play an instrument on this track. 'She's Leaving Home' is not, strictly speaking, a Beatles song at all. It is pure McCartney, from start to finish, with a little help from his friend John. And apart from their two voices, all we hear is a harp, a string nonet (four violins, two violas, two cellos and a double bass).

> **I try and make an album like a novel and then these singles are short stories.** — Paul, *South Bank Show*

Because Paul wanted to have a string section playing on the song, he rang up to ask if I could come round, take notes from him and then write up a score.

It so happened that I couldn't. I was already immersed in a recording session, with Cilla Black. Even though the Beatles were the number one thing in my life, I still had a huge roster of other artists to record. These artists understood very well that the Beatles took priority, but there were moments, and this was one of them, when I just couldn't drop everything and come running.

I was very surprised and rather hurt that Paul picked up the telephone and got hold of a fellow called Mike Leander, after I'd said I couldn't go round on the spot. Mike was a good arranger, and Paul engaged him to do the score.

Until that moment I had done everything that either Paul or the Beatles had wanted in the way of orchestration. I couldn't understand why he was so impatient all of a sudden. It obviously hadn't occurred to him that I would be upset. Years later, in fact, he said, 'I couldn't understand why it was so important to you. It was in my mind, and I wanted to get it out, get it down. That's all.'

It was just Paul being Paul.

People have been very kind to me, and said that the orchestrations I have done for Beatles songs always seemed to work, while the ones I didn't do work less well. In the event, Mike Leander did a good workmanlike job on the score of 'She's Leaving Home'; I did not change it a great deal. Twenty-odd years of hindsight make me wish I'd been tougher on it, though. At the risk of being accused of sour grapes, I find that on hearing it today, the harp part is a little bit too tinkly, the voicing of the strings a shade too lush. Could it have been a little more astringent?

My approach to writing an orchestral accompaniment has always been to keep it sparse, and to leave out anything unnecessary. It is always too easy to overdo things when you are orchestrating, on the belt and braces principle. By this I mean the 'Will this work? I'm not sure, so let's just add that to it in case it doesn't . . .' syndrome. In other words, orchestrators sometimes get a thick and heavy end result because they do not have the courage of their first conviction – that something simpler will work.

You must be very careful what note you write for a given instrument in the orchestra. What will suit the cello will not do at all for the trombone. You must also be wary not to write too many notes (as Mozart was once accused of doing) or to use too many instruments. If you can write well for a string quartet, which is what we did for 'Yesterday', you can write well for a string orchestra. A lot of people tend to think of their fingers on a piano keyboard, when they are writing for orchestra, and try to write that way for strings. You have ten fingers, though: if you have ten notes over a string orchestra, it is going to sound extremely busy, and risks sounding muddy. If you have only four notes over a string orchestra, it is likely to sound much better. After all, one note on its own sounding over an entire orchestra can be tremendously effective. I know this because Paul came to me one day and said, 'I've been listening to Beethoven, George.'

'Yeah, good, Paul,' I replied.

Ignoring my dryness, he went on: 'I've just sussed it out. You know the beginning of the Fifth Symphony? It's only unison. There are no chords. Everybody's playing the same notes!'

'You're right, Paul,' I said.

'But that's fantastic!' he enthused. 'It's a great sound!'

'Course it is,' I rejoined. 'The whole orchestra speaks with one voice – that's genius: BOM BOM BOM BO-OM! Most people probably don't even realize that it is the whole lot of them all playing single notes at once.'

We weren't doing anything like the Fifth. But I booked a small orchestra anyway: four violins, two violas, two cellos, a double-bass and a harp for Friday 17 March. The harpist was Sheila Bromberg – the first woman to appear on a Beatles record. We worked at it all evening, recording the ensemble live, and getting through eight takes trying to get it the way Paul wanted it. I filled up our first four tracks with a layout as follows:

TRACK 1: harp

TRACK 2: double-bass

TRACK 3: four violins

TRACK 4: two violas and two cellos

As we worked away in reverse roles, Paul in the control room and me in the studio directing the orchestra, I made a mental note that there was not much wrong with our first take, and Take 6 was pretty good too. In the end, we did choose Take 1 as best, so all that extra work was for nothing. To prepare for the vocals, I did a four-track-to-four-track transfer the following day, mixing the original tracks down to stereo (two tracks) on a new tape.

On the Monday we set about doing the vocals. Now that we had recorded our orchestral backing in stereo, we had only two tracks left to play with. I wanted to double-track the voices, and Paul agreed, but, because I preferred not to go to a third tape, Paul and John had to record their voices together, sharing the same track. To achieve the answering effect you get in the chorus, where Paul sings 'She . . . is leaving . . .' and John sings 'We gave her most

135

of our lives . . .' in counterpoint, the two of them had to sing their parts perfectly at the same time.

I wanted a distinct perspective on each voice, so different echoes were added to each at the time of recording. And of course I still wanted my double-tracked vocals! Once we had a good performance on Track 3, they had to sing it again exactly the same way for Track 4. Pretty hard to do, but the Beatles by this time were masters of their craft. They had had plenty of practice, over the years. We still spent most of the night on it!

'She's Leaving Home' is one of Paul's greatest. The counterpointing of the voices is economical, clear, magical. It is a song with a lovely narrative, of the type he began with 'Eleanor Rigby'. On that song, I had noticed that the phrase 'Oh, look at all the lonely people,' would work if it were sung against the end of the main tune. Counterpoint. So I suggested we did an overdub. They were knocked out with the result. 'How did you know that would work there?' Paul asked.

They themselves had an instinctive feeling for this kind of writing, requiring no spurring from me to create the two opposing lines in 'Help!', for example, which came earlier that year. But the experience of 'Eleanor Rigby' undoubtedly made Paul watch out much more actively for places to use this little trick. 'She's Leaving Home' is one of the songs where he uses counterpoint to its best effect.

In 1967 I thought that classical music was dying, or was dead. Classical music by its very nature is dead music – it is written by people who have been dead for fifty years or longer. As to 'contemporary' classical music at the time of *Pepper*, there wasn't really much of it around. There were very few living classical composers. The ones that did exist tended to be more cut off than they are now, and they were certainly poorer. It was a very closed, and a very small world. People didn't listen to avant-garde classical music in any significant numbers, so there was very little money in it. Nowadays we accept it more, people write about it and listen to it a bit more.

In 1994 there are about 1500 classical music composers in Britain who do nothing else but write classical music all day. Even today, though, most of them risk starvation. And in a population of fifty-odd million, 1500 is still not very many. It is not what you would call a widespread activity, like fishing.

Classical music conversations tend to run along the lines of, 'Have you heard Bruckner interpreted by Karajan, as opposed to Klemperer? It's most interesting . . .' The interpretation may well be interesting, but it's still Bruckner. That is all they can do with it, reweave what is already there.

Pop music, for me, was live; it was expressing what life was about, reflecting it and commenting on it, often in the best way, which is unconsciously. *Pepper* certainly does this.

Against this background, I was pretentious enough to look upon *Sgt. Pepper* as contemporary art, contemporary musical art. It had all sorts of influences, from jazz, folk music, rock 'n' roll, rhythm and blues – but it had a tremendous classical vein too. I saw the album as the first example of a new sort of music, a classical/rock crossover music that tore down the snobbery-sodden barriers that exist between the two types. I always found it ridiculous that people would refuse to listen to rock music because it was considered as 'unworthy', somehow, not as 'good' as classical music.

When we consider the Beatles' great songs, there is always one huge yawning trap we can fall into: hyperbole. It is dangerous to compare them with Schubert, because the comparison is not really between like and like. How could one compare Cole Porter with Mahler, say, or Stephen Sondheim with Chopin? All the same, 'She's Leaving Home' gets very close to that higher calibre of writing. The unfolding little drama, the everyday tragedy of ordinary folk that Paul captures in his words and music, says something truthful about a corner of suburban life. The parents' plaintive cry, 'What did we do that was wrong?' – we did our best by her, why has she gone and left us? – is touching.

The refrain is constructed almost operatically. Paul sings the higher part and John the lower, parental, voice in a telling and beautiful aria.

'She's Leaving Home' could only have been written by Paul, by this time a master songwriter. The public in Britain tend to see him now as the softy of the group, with all those lovely and love-filled songs to his credit. In truth, he was every bit as much the rocker as John, who could be just as soppy as Paul in his love songs. 'Helter Skelter', a driving rocker from Paul that was about the nearest the Beatles ever got to heavy metal, is one of so many strong examples one could pick out from their work to disprove this cliché.

John sang romantic ballads a-plenty, like 'Julia', and 'Imagine', yet he in his turn was always pigeon-holed as the rocker of the group. Paul had a gift for melody that just seemed to spring from him without effort. Time and again I would be thrilled to hear a lovely tune, with interesting harmonies, and I would wonder where it had come from. Oddly enough, Paul never knew either.

John's music was never dull, but it was for the most part monotonous in the literal sense: he liked to weave his weird and wonderful lyrics around one or two notes: 'Living is easy with eyes closed . . .'; 'Imagine there's no heaven . . .'; 'It's been a hard day's night . . .'; 'I am he as you are he, as you are me and we are all together . . .' All are monotone, or near-monotone compositions.

His cleverness came with the alterations he achieved with his harmonies, underneath the monotone. These completely transformed what might otherwise have been boring into a magnificent song. It was as though the ground shifted under one's feet. The result of this process was always intriguing, even if, as John once ruefully commented, 'You're not likely to hear "I Am The Walrus" being whistled by a waiter in a Spanish restaurant!'

Randomness as art appealed to all of the Beatles very much. The idea that a silent movie selected at random could link up with a piece of music equally randomly picked out was a great wheeze; they loved playing around like that. It's the 'Hey, wow, man, look at that' school of art, the art of the (psychedelically or otherwise) 'liberated' consciousness that was all the rage at the time. Sometimes, therefore, they would jam for hours in the studio, and we would be expected to tape it all, recognizing the moment of great genius when it came through. The only trouble was, it never did come through.

This free-form associative tinkering happened a lot after *Pepper*, on *Magical Mystery Tour*. It was a side to the Beatles that I found rather tedious. I used to say to them, 'If you want to be random, let's be organized about it,' which was definitely not what they wanted to hear when they were in that mood. But they would just about put up with it, from me.

When John brought along 'I Am The Walrus', later in 1967, I said, 'I see what you're trying to get out: it's very bizarre, but it's great. Let's organize it.' John went along with that. I wrote out a score for cellos, wrote out all the parts for the singers, right down to the 'ha ha has' and the 'hee hee hees' which John had suggested, sung by the Mike Sammes Singers.

Weirdness was fine by me, in fact I loved the anarchy of John's thoughts – if I could fix and channel them. And the random could occasionally work wonders. John thought of adding completely random sounds to our mix of 'I Am The Walrus'. He took a leaf out of John Cage's book, who long before had used a radio broadcast to create a 'happening'. So we had a radio brought in, hooked it up to the recording console, and gave John the tuning knob to twiddle. In no time, he found what he wanted: a Shakespeare play, *King Lear*, in full flow, going out live. It was by then so late in the evening that we were probably the only people listening to Will's drama: but it went into the mix all the same, and is there now for ever.

I thought John had liked all the production techniques we had pioneered on *Pepper*, but no sooner was it finished than he rebelled against them. He wanted to get back to what he called 'honesty', in recording – in other words, he wanted to make them as near to live performances as possible. I reckoned we were making little movies in sound, not stage plays. If a little artifice gave a better result, why not use it? After all, we were honest and up front about the tricks we used.

I was saying to them then, 'Think symphonically; think of themes that you can bring back in different keys; think of counterpoint; think of putting one song against another song, so that each gives something extra to the other – there are all sorts of things you can do.' But John would have none of it.

'That's not rock 'n' roll to me, George,' he said. 'Rock 'n' roll is grooving to a good song.'

Paul, on the other hand, really took to the notion of the 'seamless symphony', if I can call it that, which we had come up with for *Pepper*. This is why *Abbey Road* has a side of what John wanted, the very distinct individual tracks like 'Come Together', 'Something', and even 'Octopus's Garden' on side one; while Paul and I got a much more continuous work, in the style of *Pepper*, on side two: 'Because', 'You Never Give Me Your Money', 'Sun King', and so on. The 'Golden Slumbers' sequence to the end of the record remains one of my favourite tracks.

By the time we came to do *Abbey Road*, the madness years were over, and John was happy to help us with the second side of the album: he wrote quite a bit of it! 'Because' is one of his masterpieces. No, there were no problems, but he still preferred his out-and-out 'rockers'.

Long after John died, Yoko said to me, 'I wish you'd worked with John on his last album – it would have been so much better.' I thought *Double Fantasy* was pretty damn good as it was. 'Well,' I replied, 'you didn't ask me!' But I was surprised and rather touched that she really believed that.

CHAPTER SEVENTEEN

'What do you see when you turn out the light?'

Paul and John wrote 'With A Little Help From My Friends' especially for Ringo. But the tradition that Ringo always had a song to sing on an album was nothing to do with the others being kind to him. Perched up behind his drums at the back of the stage, Ringo occupied a special place in the hearts of many Beatles fans. The most common adjectives you heard about him were 'cute', and 'cuddly'. Having him sing something on every album, then, was extremely good marketing – simple as that.

Ringo was definitely not interested in singing the words, 'Would you stand up and throw tomatoes at me . . .' which is how the second line of this song originally went. So Paul and John had to change it to 'Would you stand up and walk out on me.' It was bad enough, as Ringo quite rightly pointed out, that they were pelted half to death on stage with jelly-babies, after George confided a liking for them in an unguarded interview. But if the fans started throwing tomatoes . . .!

'A Little Help From My Friends' was designed to flow out of the album's title song, 'Sgt. Pepper's Lonely Hearts Club Band'. By the time they came to write it, the idea of an alternative Beatles, of a make-believe band in which they could be what they wanted to be, had taken firm hold. Their 'Billy Shears' character was another stab at making the whole *Pepper* idea a bit more real, giving it a bit of solid flesh. The obvious person to be this Billy Shears, then, was Ringo – it was somehow his kind of song.

Work on 'Bad Finger Boogie', its original, working title, began on 29 March. The boys had booked the studio for 7 p.m., as usual, but on this occasion they arrived really late. They had been off doing the photograph for the *Pepper* album cover, at Chelsea

Manor studios in Flood Street. They turned up at about 11 p.m.

With this song Paul and John had really come up with the goods. Ringo's voice is extremely distinctive, warm and memorable – but he would be the last person to claim that it has much range. So Paul wrote a beautifully simple melody for him, again based around no more than five notes. All Ringo's voice had to carry was one little phrase:

Terribly simple, terribly effective. Economy is the mark of genius.

I played the smidgin of Hammond organ that underscores the 'Billy Shears' introduction just before the song proper begins. Paul played piano, George lead guitar and Ringo drums. Nothing unusual in that. For this track, though, John was relegated to cow-bell.

TRACK 1: piano – Paul
TRACK 2: guitar – George
TRACK 3: drums – Ringo
         cow-bell – John
TRACK 4: empty

We put down the piano, guitar and drums that night, transferring them to another four-track tape. Next day, 30 March, we added more of George's lead guitar, Paul's bass guitar line and Ringo's tambourine. They had to play together, because all this went on to a single track of the new tape. We recorded John and Paul's superb backing vocals next, before we got to Ringo's solo voice, throwing in a tad more guitar from George on to these vocal tracks for good measure.

John could be insecure about his voice; but Ringo made John look brazenly confident. Regardless of the lyrics, Ringo was extremely diffident about singing such a major piece, as he saw it. Paul and John coaxed him and cajoled him; and in the end, they sang along with him when he did his stuff. It was a brilliant three-way live performance, that recording.

In the last seconds of 'A Little Help From My Friends', when he had to hit the last, dangerously high note, Ringo did it wonderfully well. It is one of the best performances he ever turned in, perhaps the best track he has ever sung. Though we had worked all night, from 11 p.m. until 7 a.m., it was worth it. He came up trumps.

He really was Billy Shears.

If George had a slight burden to carry in being the Third Man within the group, Ringo had the burden, initially at least, of being the 'replacement' man. To this day Ringo has never forgiven me for not allowing him to play on his first Beatles recording session. He joked about it when we were shooting the *South Bank Show* documentary about *Pepper*, in 1993, but beneath that joking was the feeling that I shouldn't have done it, that I should have let him play.

The incident dates back thirty-one years, to 1962, and yet it still makes a little wave when we meet! It is amazing how these things persist.

There are two versions of 'Love Me Do': the single which did feature Ringo on drums, and the album version, which had Andy White on drums, and Ringo playing tambourine. It wasn't until the issue of a 'rarities' album in the United States that Ringo's drumming saw the light of day.

In retrospect I can understand how bitter he must have felt about his recording debut with the band, but it was all down to communication, or rather lack of it. On the 6 June Beatles' session I decided that Pete Best had to go. I said to Brian Epstein, 'I don't care what you do with Pete Best; he is not playing on any more recording sessions. I'm getting a session drummer in, because above all else these guys need a good drummer.'

I was not aware that in the meantime the other three Beatles had arrived at the same conclusion, although not necessarily for the same reason; Brian had somehow neglected to tell me. He may, of course, have been as ignorant as I was.

So for that first recording session I had booked a top session drummer, Andy White, as a replacement for Pete.

When Ringo turned up, I wondered who the hell he was. When I found out he expected to be the drummer on the track, I jibbed at this second possibility of losing a good driving beat for the band, and insisted that Andy play. I had never met Ringo before, and obviously hadn't the slightest idea whether he was good, bad or indifferent. And I wasn't going to waste precious studio time finding out. Consolation prize for Ringo was tambourine! (By the way, my own version of events differs again slightly here from some accounts. My diary shows that I did not oversee any Beatles recording sessions on 11 September – only the one on 4 September.)

Later, I did get him to play, and I realized he was excellent. But it was hardly the best way to get off on the right foot.

There is nothing in life quite like good communication.

Ringo always got and still gets a unique sound out of his drums, a sound as distinctive as his voice. This was slammed home to me in Montserrat, many years later, when Paul came out to record *Tug of War* in my own AIR studio. Ringo agreed to play drums on the album, and we also engaged a New York-based session drummer, one of the very best of modern drummers, Steve Gadd. Steve is a very clean and enormously precise drummer, a great technical performer. We had Steve and Ringo playing drums together on one track, same microphone set-up, but they had their own drum-kits.

The difference in sound was quite amazing. Ringo gets a looser, deeper sound out of his drums that is unique. Quite often, because Ringo wanted his bass drum to sound deeper still, we would have to alter the tape-speed. This detailed attention to the tone of his drums is one of the reasons for Ringo's brilliance. Another is that although Ringo does not keep time with metronome accuracy, he has an unrivalled feel for a song. If his timing fluctuates it invariably does so in the right place at the right time, keeping the right atmosphere going on the track and giving it a rock-solid foundation. This held true for every single Beatles number on which he played.

I was a very big Beatles fan, and each album they made they upped themselves, especially with and after *Rubber Soul*. *Sgt. Pepper*, for one thing, was the album that changed drumming more than anything else. Before that album, drum 'fills' in rock 'n' roll were pretty rudimentary, all much the same, and this record had what I call space fills where they would leave a tremendous amount of air. It was most appealing to me musically. Also the sound of the drums got much better. What I had to figure out now

was: What am I going to do to get drums to sound like that?
— Al Kooper, of Blood, Sweat and Tears

Ringo was also a great tom-tom player. 'A Day In The Life' features Ringo heavily on the toms, and is probably his best performance on the album, or anywhere in the recordings he did for the Beatles. Most of the other tracks on *Pepper* include tom-toms somewhere, too.

But the most remarkable thing Ringo has is this unique and very funny way of looking at the world. He is the absolute master of the one-liner. During the making of the *Pepper* television film in 1993 I wanted to give a little credit to our engineer, Geoff Emerick. In 1956 he was very young; he'd been thrown right in at the deep end and had to cope with some very complicated recording. He came on board when Norman 'Hurricane' Smith gave up being the Beatles' engineer following the release of *Rubber Soul*.

Geoff gave us wonderful service, making sure that the tapes were well-engineered during innumerable all-night sessions. When people say to me, 'How did you ever manage to record *Pepper* using only four-track tape recorders?' I answer glibly, 'With great difficulty.'

The truth is that had Geoff Emerick not been Geoff Emerick – and managed to stay awake during all of those overnight sessions – the quality of those tapes could easily have been bloody awful. I reckon he deserves a lot of credit for that. The Beatles, though, did not really see how important Geoff was. They certainly did not appreciate that he was a fundamental part of the team. During filming, when we asked Ringo, 'Have you got any memories of Geoff Emerick?' he answered, 'Yeah. He sweated a lot.'

The studio manager called me to his office and asked whether I'd like to be the Beatles' engineer. That took me a little bit by surprise! In fact it terrified me. I remember playing a game in my head, eeny, meeny, miney, mo, yes, no, shall I say yes, shall I say no?
— Geoff Emerick, *South Bank Show*

Ringo's quirky vision comes out particularly in his use of language. Everyone knows that the title 'A Hard Day's Night' was taken from a Ringo comment at the end of a particularly gruelling overnight session. But 'Tomorrow Never Knows' was his title, too. It was just the way his mind worked – with a little twist that could make a brilliant difference.

> **Well I think he's vastly underrated, Ringo. The drum fills on 'A Day In The Life' were in fact very, very complex things. You could take a great drummer from today and say, 'I want it like that,' and they wouldn't know what to do . . .'**
>
> – Phil Collins, *South Bank Show*

CHAPTER EIGHTEEN

'It's getting very near the end . . .'

The reprise of 'Sgt. Pepper's Lonely Hearts Club Band' was another Neil Aspinall brainwave. 'You've given a concert,' he commented. 'Why don't you wrap up the concert with another version of "Sgt. Pepper"?' Everyone thought that was a great idea. So, on 20 April, that was what we did.

This time, we really went hammer and tongs for a live performance. This version of the song is much better – up-tempo, faster, pulsating with energy, much livelier. The Beatles knew the song inside out by now, and there was a sort of end-of-term feeling in the studio. We had never made a second recording of a song on an album before, and that was exciting in itself. We finished the whole recording – vocals, solos, the lot – in one overnight session of eleven hours' straight work, from seven in the evening until six o'clock the next morning.

We were in the big studio at Abbey Road, No.1, for this one, and the natural acoustics of this vast, cavernous room lent something to the live, bright quality of that recording. Geoff Emerick had a problem sorting out the balance between the various vocal and instrumental inputs, but he fixed it, and the electrifying, football stadium atmosphere comes through.

We had to use an isolation booth for the heavy stuff – that is, we had to shut away the drums in a sort of portable, sound-absorbing cabinet. Had we not done that, the recording would have been a cacophony, the instruments spilling into one another as though being played in a cathedral.

Remarkably, we recorded the whole song on one four-track tape only:

TRACK 1: rhythm and lead guitar

TRACK 2: bass guitar

TRACK 3: vocals

TRACK 4: drums and percussion

Nine takes. Four false starts. Five performances. No overdubs. Take five was marked best.

For the first time on a Beatles album, Paul's bass guitar was recorded not with a microphone and an amplifier, but through a direct injection box, plugged directly from his guitar into the recording board. It was a lash-up, cobbled together by our unsung behind-the-scenes technical genius, Ken Townsend. DI was a first for us, a real breakthrough. It meant we could 'cook' the bass guitar any way we wanted.

Always one for a novelty, John said, 'Hey, that's gear; why don't we do that to all our instruments? In fact, I'd like to sing like that!'

'Well, John,' I replied, 'we could inject your voice directly into the board; but there is just one small thing: you'll have to have a minor surgical operation to implant a jack-plug into your neck...'

We reconvened the next night, recording a master vocal from Paul, together with the backing voices on to Track 3. And that was it: done, in a twinkling.

The reprise was a neat way of rounding off the original concept: 'OK, you've had your show, now it's time to go...'

We had an album.

The running order of the songs on the finished album was pretty much left to me to decide, with the Beatles giving final approval. We had to start with the song that gave the illusion of a concept, 'Sgt. Pepper's Lonely Hearts Club Band'; that has to be the first track, naturally. The reprise of this song, for the same reason, had to go last – except that the final chord of 'A Day In The Life' was so final that it was obvious nothing else could follow it. So the reprise of 'Sgt. Pepper's Lonely Hearts Club Band' was put back to second to last. That took care of three of our tracks already.

My old precept in the recording business was always 'Make side one strong,' for obvious commercial reasons. Since the last line of 'Sgt. Pepper's Lonely Hearts Club Band' introduces the fictional 'Billy Shears' (i.e. one Ringo Starr), 'A Little Help From My

Friends' had to come immediately after the title track. Four down.

'Lucy In The Sky With Diamonds' was a great song: it had to go on side one. It could hardly be more different in atmosphere and mood from 'A Little Help From My Friends', so why place it after that? Well, it was because it was so different. It was a complete change of musical colour, which was welcome. It was like saying, 'Here's a green show,' with the first two tracks, then the lights went down, and suddenly up comes a red show. You wanted a change there; you wanted to hear something really different. The phrase that opens 'Lucy' is a great hook, very evocative, and coming here in the running order it cools the rather hot beginning right down.

Another principle of mine when assembling an album was always to go out on a side strongly, placing the weaker material towards the end but then going out with a bang. With this in mind, 'Being For The Benefit Of Mr. Kite' ends side one.

The songs that were least interesting had to come before that and after 'Lucy'. 'She's Leaving Home' was a lovely song, but it was a bit downbeat – it didn't exactly shout its optimism – so I decided to place it after the more upbeat but less worthy 'Fixing A Hole' and 'Getting Better'. These were all entirely subjective judgements, of course!

When it came to 'Within You Without You', I could not for the life of me think of anywhere to put it at all. It was so alien, mystical and long. There was no way it could end a side, nor did it sit comfortably next to anything else on the album. The self-deprecating laugh George had added at the end of his song gave me a bizarre idea: it could start a side, and I could follow it with a jokey track: 'When I'm Sixty-Four'.

A lot of people like 'Lovely Rita', but it was not my favourite song, as I've said, so that one went into the middle of side two as a bit of padding. 'Good Morning, Good Morning' found its place by virtue of a happy accident, when I noticed that the chicken squawk on the end of the song dovetailed, or rather could be made to dovetail, neatly with the sound of the guitar tuning-up that begins the title song's reprise. Finally came the big blockbuster that ends the album, 'A Day In The Life': nothing could come after that final, numbing, 42-second chord.

When we were putting the album together at the end, it struck me that we had such a funny collection of songs, not really related to one another, all disparate numbers. Looking them over, I really did start to worry that we were being a bit pretentious, a bit clever-clever.

What helped me have confidence in the album was that the imperious Alan Livingston, the head of Capitol Records, flew over to London to find out what we were up to. This was just after we had finished recording 'A Day In The Life'.

This sudden visitation from on high came well after Livingston's company had turned down the Beatles three times, when we had been trying to break into the US market some three years earlier. The Capitol label agreed to sign the Beatles only at our fourth attempt, when their success could no longer be denied – or resisted.

Each rejection came without a word of apology – no 'Sorry, guys,' – only the 'reasons', consistently given: 'They would not sell in America,' and, 'Believe me, we know our market better than you do.' Suddenly, now that the Beatles had become stratospherically successful, it was all 'I want you to meet my boys . . .' stuff from Livingston. He regarded the success of the Beatles in the US as his own.

I played him 'A Day In The Life'. It knocked him sideways. He was completely flabbergasted by it. He was in no way perturbed by any aspect of the song, by its relatively bizarre lyrics or its avant-garde production – only speechless with admiration.

I knew then that we were home and dry.

I suppose I had been worried that we might be leaving our public behind, getting a bit too fast in front. If Alan Livingston liked it, though . . .

If we had not given away 'Strawberry Fields Forever' and 'Penny Lane' for the double-A-sided single of 1966, but had included them on *Pepper*, what would we have dropped from the album instead? Maybe 'Within You Without You', but that would have broken the golden rule that George Harrison always had one of his songs on an album. So it would have to have been 'Lovely Rita' and 'When I'm Sixty-Four'. It's fun to imagine what a re-edited *Sgt. Pepper's Lonely Hearts Club Band* with those two crackers on it might be like!

When it came to compiling the album, I tried to edit it together in a very tight format, and in a funny kind of way when I was editing it it almost grew by itself; it took on a life of its own.

CHAPTER NINETEEN

1 June 1967:
'Their production will be
second to none . . .'

The album was released on the first day of June. With the 'failure' of 'Strawberry Fields Forever' and 'Penny Lane' on the previous year's Christmas market fresh in our minds, we all held our breath to see what the reaction to it would be. Would it sell? Would the critics savage it? I was downright scared, but not half as worried as the Beatles. John and Paul in particular were on the telephone to Tony Barrow, the Beatles' press officer, all the time: 'Had advance copies of *Pepper* been sent out to the radio stations in time? Would it be a good idea if they were to dress up in *Pepper* gear and false beards and march on Buckingham Palace with a brass band playing behind them? Would that attract enough publicity?' They were full of ideas like this for crazy stunts, a symptom of their nervousness.

We were apprehensive that we had gone too far with *Pepper*; too far and too fast, that is, for the buying public and the critics. Five per cent of me was thinking, 'This is never going to work, we've been too pretentious, it's all too complicated and uncommercial, far too different from what the Beatles have done before.' The other ninety-five per cent of me was thinking, 'This is brilliant! They're going to love it!'

We worried needlessly, as things turned out. *Pepper* sold 250,000 copies in the first week of going on sale in the UK. Within one month, it had sold more than 500,000 copies. By the end of August it had sold over two-and-a-half million copies in the United States. In Britain, it stayed at number one in the album charts for twenty-seven weeks, in the US for nineteen weeks . . . It just kept on selling and selling.

Instead of going for a massive, all-singing and dancing press-launch extravaganza for the album's release, Brian decided on a 'listen-in', as it inevitably got called, at his Chapel Street flat. A select few journalists and friends were invited along, and it was the hottest ticket in town. Brian laid on copious quantities of fine food and drink, and played *Sgt. Pepper* at full volume for the duration of the feast.

Writing in the 27 May 1967 edition of *Melody Maker*, journalist Jack Hutton described the scene as he surveyed the merry gathering thus:

> **Downstairs, a long genuine antique table groaned, as they say, under huge dishes of cold meats and vegetables served by white-jacketed waiters.**
>
> **To drink there was a choice of gazpacho, a cold soup, or champers. The champers won handsomely.**

> **Yellow Socks**
>
> **The boys were in fine fettle. Lennon won the sartorial stakes with a green flower-patterned shirt, red cord trousers, yellow socks and what looked like cord shoes.**
>
> **His ensemble was completed by a sporran. With his bushy sideboards and National Health specs he resembled an animated Victorian watchmaker.**
>
> **Paul McCartney, sans moustache, wore a loosely tied scarf over a shirt, a striped double-breasted jacket and looked like someone out of a Scott Fitzgerald novel.**

The music critics, where they could make any sense at all of the new album, reacted in ways that were as diverse as the songs featured on it. But they were generally favourable. Under the headline: 'The Beatles revive hopes of progress in pop music,' William Mann, music critic of *The Times* newspaper, said:

> **Any of these songs is more genuinely creative than anything currently to be heard on pop radio stations, but in relationship to what other groups have been doing lately *Sgt. Pepper* is chiefly significant as constructive criticism, a sort of pop music master class examining trends and correcting or tidying up inconsistencies and undisciplined work, here and there suggesting a line worth following . . .'**

Allen Evans, of the *New Musical Express*, commented, 'Whether the album is their best yet, I wouldn't like to say after one hearing. Whether it was worth the five months it took to make, I would argue. But it is a very good LP, and will sell like hot cakes . . .'

Writing in the *Sunday Times*, Derek Jewell said,

The new L.P. *Sgt. Pepper's Lonely Hearts Club Band* is remarkable. Listening to its strange cadences, the sitar passages, its almost atonal propensities, the learned critic might easily assume derivations ranging from English 17th Century music to Richard Strauss . . . But the influences are likelier to be music hall artists of the last twenty-five years, and the images which Lennon and McCartney retain of their Liverpool childhood – of places, priests, old women, young girls . . .

**   *Pepper* is a tremendous advance even in the increasingly adventurous progress of the Beatles. Some of the words are splendid urban poetry – almost metaphysical in 'Lucy in the Sky with Diamonds'. The tone is humorous, sympathetic, sceptical and often self-mocking. Musically, it is always stimulating. There won't, though, be much dancing done to *Pepper*. The Beatles are now producing performances, not music for frugging to. Will the kids follow?**

The *New Statesman*'s Wilfred Mellers opined,

The new Beatle L.P. *Sgt. Pepper's Lonely Hearts Club Band* continues the trend initiated in *Revolver* and *Penny Lane*; though it starts from the conventions of pop it becomes 'art' – and art of an increasingly subtle kind. For one thing the beautifully produced disc isn't just a collection of numbers but a whole of which the parts, if remarkably various, are related. This whole is about loneliness; and the period comedy of *Sgt. Pepper's Lonely Hearts Club Band*,

153

which begins as a hilarious evocation of old-style (Edwardian?) camaraderie, is gradually transformed as the 'lonely' elements are detached from the hearts, the club and the band – the things that make us simple, social creatures.

Mark Lewisohn, British Beatles guru, said of it:

Millions of words have been written about this LP, almost every one fulsome in its praise, but what surely stands out most of all is the Beatles' sheer progression to this point in time. Here were four musicians, raw and inexperienced in June 1962, changing popular music right-about-face by June 1967.

It had an amazing effect on the way people saw records. It opened a door and showed everybody that there was another room; that you could play around in that room, and yet it would still be called a commercial record.

– Phil Collins

It was Stateside, though, that the critics really let rip. Here is US writer Langdon Winner:

At the time *Sgt. Pepper* was released I happened to be driving across country on Interstate 80. In each city where I stopped for gas or food – Laramie, Ogallala, Moline, South Bend – the melodies wafted in from some far-off transistor radio or portable hi-fi. It was the most amazing thing I've ever heard. For a brief moment, the irreparably fragmented consciousness of the West was unified, at least in the minds of the young . . .

Jack Kroll, in *Newsweek*, 26 June 1967, went equally far: '*Sgt. Pepper* is such an organic work . . .' he wrote,

that it is like a pop *Façade,* the suite of poems by Edith Sitwell musicalized by William Walton. Like *Façade,*

154

Sgt. Pepper is a rollicking, probing language-and-sound vaudeville, which grafts skin from all three brows – high, middle and low – into a pulsating collage about mid-century manners and madness . . .

The new Beatles are justified by the marvelous last number alone, 'A Day In The Life', which was foolishly banned by the BBC because of its refrain 'I'd love to turn you on.' But this line means many things, coming as it does after a series of beautifully sorrowful stanzas in which John confronts the world's incessant bad news, sighing 'Oh boy' with a perfect blend of innocence and spiritual exhaustion. Evoking the catatonic metropolitan crowd (like Eliot's living dead flowing across London Bridge), John's wish to 'turn you on' is a desire to start the bogged-down juices of life itself. This point is underscored by an overwhelming musical effect, using a 41-piece orchestra – a growling, bone-grinding crescendo that drones up like a giant crippled turbine struggling to spin new power into a foundered civilization. This number is the Beatles' *Waste Land,* a superb achievement of their brilliant and startlingly effective popular art.

Alan Ginsberg described *Pepper* as, 'A towering modern opera . . .'

It may have met with a good reception from most fans and commentators, but even so there were voices hostile to the new release. One Richard Goldstein, a writer on the *New York Village Voice*, gave the following reactions: 'Like the cover, the overall effect is busy, hip and cluttered. An obsession with production, coupled with a surprising shoddiness in composition, permeates the entire album. A package of special effects, dazzling but ultimately fraudulent.' Ouch, that hurt!

The most spectacular and extreme reaction came from the British Broadcasting Corporation. To this day I still can't understand why the BBC banned 'A Day In The Life'. I think if the track had just been a rhythm track, conventionally recorded, no one would have taken any notice. But the anarchic sound of the orchestral climax seems to have contributed to the idea that the song's lyrics meant something nasty, something sinister: subversive even, at the very least an encouragement to take drugs. The vocal wailings in the bridge of the song definitely contributed to its reception as a 'marijuana dream'. To us, though, those vocals were no more than an inventive way of getting back to the original key!

When the controversy over 'A Day In The Life' really got going the British press surpassed itself, reading all kinds of sinister hidden meanings into that and other *Pepper* songs. The newspapers fed the frenzy by looking endlessly for drug allusions, not just seizing on 'Lucy In The Sky With Diamonds' as a supposed acronym for LSD, but harping away on a persistent line of innuendo that the whole album was drug-inspired, adding fuel to the BBC's already near-hysterical stance.

It was suggested, for example, that 'Four thousand holes in Blackburn, Lancashire' was a reference to puncture marks in the skin from injecting heroin. Auntie BBC was only too ready to swallow this. In fact, as I've said, it was just another article from the *Daily Mail*'s 'Far & Near' column (one of John's strangest Muses), which he had noticed while trying to compose one day.

As for 'Fixing A Hole', well that was obviously about shooting up the deadly drug, wasn't it? No use Paul protesting otherwise, that it was just about a hole in the roof where the rain gets in: 'If you're a junkie sitting in a room fixing a hole then that's what it will mean to you, but when I wrote it I meant if there's a crack or the room is uncolourful, then I'll paint it.'

Even Paul's innocuous line, 'When are you free to take some tea with me?' – this timid little clerk's enquiry to a meter maid he wants to date – was awarded sinister druggy overtones. Commentators assumed that 'tea' here meant dope, as it sometimes did in Stateside hippy-speak, rather than the domestically drinkable, common-or-garden Indian stuff you add hot water to. Absurd. But a lot of people believed this kind of stuff then. A few still do. (Come to that, there were some people who condemned Frank Sinatra's classic 'Strangers In The Night' as a statement of homosexual love.)

If you do anything different in art, something unexpected, people tend to look beyond the work for a reason with which to damn it. There is a persistent element in the great British Establishment that thinks, 'If anything is radically new, it must be a threat, it's out to undermine us and our whole national way of life. Ban it.'

Really, the fuss over possible drug connotations was a continuation of an attitude that was clearly expressed in the group's early days. Speaking in a House of Lords debate on the 'problem' of leisure in May 1964, Labour peer Ted Willis had this to say about the music of the Beatles: 'primitive . . .' having the same function 'as the war dances of savage and backward people . . . phoney . . . a ritual pep pill, a cheap, plastic, candyfloss substitute for culture'. Lord Taylor, in reply, was moved to defend the group in these terms: 'I personally do not think it is wicked to like the Beatles.'

The then Minister of Information, Sir William Deedes, was kinder, and more accurate: 'They [the Beatles] herald a cultural movement among the young which may become part of the history of our times . . .'

Thirty years down the road there is no longer any debate – the cultural barricades have been stormed. With *Sgt. Pepper's Lonely Hearts Club Band*, as with all their music, the Beatles helped to shift the entire focus of modern British culture. Now, for good or ill, pop culture has swallowed society whole.

Despite the controversy over drugs, *Sgt. Pepper's Lonely Hearts Club Band* caught people's imagination more than any other Beatles album. It was not just that it was a good album, that it was different and couldn't be reproduced live, all that kind of thing. There was nothing comparable to it around at the time, and it was seen as a complete breakthrough, as an album that set a new standard. It was acceptable as the first 'concept' album, even though it was not really one.

In fact, its enormous success was to have unfortunate consequences in succeeding years, when some truly awful 'concept' albums in the style of *Pepper* got taken very seriously indeed by people who should have known better.

But what it did do was succeed in speaking for its age, capturing the sixties and much of what that era came to stand for in sound: the psychedelia, the fashions, the vogue for Eastern mysticism, the spirit of adventure, the whole peace and love thing, the anti-war movement; it was all there and more. *Pepper* isn't the best thing the Beatles ever did, musically speaking. It is arguably the most important. This album did for the sixties what Frank Sinatra did for

Swinging Lovers a decade earlier – but with knobs on. It liberated, in song, the dreams and ideals of a generation.

Over the weeks, months and years since its release, it has been a bit like watching iron-filings falling into a pattern round a magnet: *Pepper*, somehow, has become the sixties. It has been the most extraordinary thing to watch.

Pepper spawned myth upon myth, it fed on itself. The myth of Paul being dead, because his back was turned on the back cover photograph of the album, is typical of how it came to be viewed. An aura of mysticism grew up around the album, which we inadvertently fed, because of the silly things we did messing about: the high-pitched whistle on the end of the recording, audible only to dogs, for example, which people thought must mean something deep, certainly something mysterious. Actually, the 20,000-hertz tone went on the end of the album after I had been explaining to the blokes how there were certain frequencies that human beings could not hear. I mentioned that dogs, however, were able to hear much higher frequences than we could. Inevitably, this prompted Paul to say, jokingly, 'You realize we never record anything for animals, don't you? What about my dog, Martha? Let's put on something only a dog can hear.'

Or again, the silly nonsense we taped on to the run-out groove at the very end of the record, which turned into something 'rude' if you played it backwards. Actually, we mumbled a few words into tape, cut the tape up, and recorded the result backwards. The bizarre nature of the sleeve, Jann Haworth's cut-outs, the moustaches, the sergeant's stripes and so on that came inside the original album ... all this stoked the fires of public and press imagination.

It is ironic that the last Beatles concert should have taken place in Candlestick Park, San Francisco, when that city's Bay Area gave birth to the whole drugs counter-culture in the first place. There is no doubt that the experience of taking drugs, and in particular LSD, was one of the main reasons why groups like the Beatles moved the pop song away from the old three-minute rock 'n' roll formula to a much more experimental, much freer musical form. 'Tomorrow Never Knows' or 'Within You Without You' could hardly have been more different from 'She Loves You' if they'd tried. This holds good for nearly all of the songs on *Pepper*. If the

Beatles as a live touring group died in San Francisco, *Sgt. Pepper* was born there.

If the Beatles' professional career were to be plotted on a graph, then *Pepper* would be the high point. *Rubber Soul* and *Revolver* were also peaks. *Magical Mystery Tour* was a definite dip. *The Beatles* (the so-called 'White Album') was a straight line on the graph, a plateau, extremely accomplished and different in its own way, but not as unified as any of the other albums in terms of overall sound. *Let It Be* was also a bit of a down slope on the graph, whereas *Abbey Road* was a lift, a great album, which I prefer to *Pepper*. Somehow, though, none of these other albums, great or good, has ever attained the status of *Pepper*.

Although we had been concerned about reaction to the album, we didn't just sit around chewing our blankets, waiting to see what would happen. *Pepper* had set the Beatles' creative energies bubbling, so we plunged headlong into more recording: first the beginnings of *Magical Mystery Tour*, then in no time at all, we were on world-wide television live singing 'All You Need Is Love'.

If *Sgt. Pepper* was the definitive hippy symphony, 'All You Need Is Love' was the hippy anthem par excellence; its message is positive; in fact it is viciously idealistic. It is John Lennon, in full awareness of the power of television and popular music as the means of mass communication, putting over his vision of a universe free of war, hatred, poverty and problems. The song presents the possibility of a perfect world, and insists on the ripeness for change of the very imperfect world he saw around him, on its willingness to change. It is an extremely simple song, written around a six-note span, its message correspondingly direct.

'All You Need Is Love' came out just after *Pepper*, as the UK's contribution to the BBC's *Our World* television programme. Transmitted by satellite on Sunday, 25 June 1967, *Our World* was the world's first-ever globally networked television show. It was seen by an estimated 400 million people: not quite the 1.5 billion who watched the first *Live Aid* concert in 1985, but pretty awesome for its day. The BBC press release said *Our World* was, for the first time ever, 'linking five continents and bringing man face to face with mankind, in places as far apart as Canberra and Cape Kennedy, Moscow and Montreal, Samarkand and Söderfors, Takamatsu and Tunis.' Phew!

The huge success of the Beatles' live performance of 'All You Need Is Love' on that show is important. It shows how they had become, in the words of the little rhyme John had long ago composed to keep up group morale on those endless drives to dreary dance-halls, 'the toppermost of the poppermost'.

> JOHN: 'Where are we going, fellas?'
> CHORUS: 'To the top, Johnny, to the TOP!'
> JOHN: 'And where is the top, fellas?'
> CHORUS: 'To the toppermost of the poppermost!'

Important, too, is the fact that the Beatles were the automatic choice to represent Britain world-wide.

'All You Need Is Love' is the swan song of this golden period for the Beatles, their time of innocence, their time of happiness, their time of ultimate success. Musically and philosophically, then, it is of a piece with its immediate precursor: *Sgt. Pepper's Lonely Hearts Club Band*.

It was the time, the attitude, it was the concept. The world was trying to change; it didn't quite make it; but it made a small move. — Ringo, *South Bank Show*

For me personally that broadcast came at the end of a crazy and terrible seven days. Judy and I had moved that week, from the tiny little flat we had, a space we knew would be entirely unsuitable for the child that was about to appear. I'd saved up all the money I'd been paid for the music to the film *A Hard Day's Night* and put it as down-payment on a house just off Hyde Park Square. We moved in on the Saturday, 24 June.

My father, a marvellous old man of eighty-four, who had been fit all his life, had been taken into hospital on the previous weekend with a chest complaint. I had been going in to see him every day, and he seemed to be getting along fine. He was weak, but in good spirits. On the morning of 20 June I turned up to visit him in hospital as usual. As I went into the ward, the sister called me aside.

'I'm afraid your father died early this morning,' she said. And that was it. A whole part of my life gone, in a sentence. I could not believe it. I stumbled out, blinded by tears. All you need is love.

CHAPTER TWENTY

Epilogue:
'Life flows on within you
and without you . . .'

**After Brian died we all collapsed ... That was the
disintegration.**
— John Lennon Remembers

I knew as *Pepper* was coming to a close that it was the end of a
chapter in our lives. Judy, my wife, who had been pregnant all this
time, needed a holiday as much as I did. We left Britain on 12 May,
despite the fact that the Beatles wanted to, and did, record 'All
Together Now', with Geoff Emerick looking after them in my
absence. We set off in our little Triumph Herald for France and
Italy, and had a lovely holiday buzzing about by the sea. We were a
day late getting back, coming home to all the furore of the album's
release on 1 June.

After working during June on 'Magical Mystery Tour' and 'All
You Need Is Love' we had the blessed relief of a break in Beatles
recordings during July. 'Relief' because I could give a bit more time
and energy to further drastic upheavals in my personal life. Our first
child, Lucie, was born on 9 August. Judy was fine, and was back
home within a week.

Little Lucie, however, being slightly premature, had to remain
in hospital for a while. So in August my time was spent rushing
between St Thomas's and Abbey Road studios, where I was doing
bits and bobs on 'Your Mother Should Know'. After a couple of
weeks of this we were allowed to take Lucie home.

I knew the boys were off to Wales, to meet up with the
Maharishi. So it was with great joy that we found ourselves able to
go to the country, with Lucie in our arms for the first time, that

weekend, 25 August. It was a marvellous place, far from the madding crowd but not exactly overflowing with mod cons. We had no phone in our cottage.

On the Sunday we strolled up the lane to have a pre-lunch drink in the village pub. It fell silent as we walked in. We knew straight away that something was wrong. The proprietor leaned over to me: 'Your friend's died,' he murmured.

'What?' I replied. I had no idea what he was talking about.

'Epstein,' he said. 'Brian Epstein.'

Both Judy and I were shattered. Brian had been one of our closest friends. Though there had been a few ups and downs professionally, we had been a happy trio when we had been able to spend time with him. He was pretty much part of the family.

When we married, in 1966, Brian gave a dinner party for us at his house in Charles Street, just behind Hyde Park Corner. All four Beatles came, with wives and girlfriends, but Brian had no one, so we were eleven to dinner.

As we started dinner, everyone took out their napkins. Brian looked around the table and said, 'Now, everyone, when you finish the meal, I want you to pass all your napkin rings back to Judy and George, because you'll see on them . . .' He broke off, and looked at us with pleased anticipation. We looked at the little rings. Each had an 'M' engraved on it. We still have the eleven silver rings, to celebrate the eleven of us at dinner.

It was a lovely thing to do. But he was like that: immensely generous, imaginative and impulsive. I stood there, in the pub, not really seeing or hearing anything. The idea that he was dead now, suddenly, without warning: it just wouldn't sink in.

I couldn't understand why he should be dead. He had been pretty much alive the last time I had seen him, and he was quite a young man. It was inexplicable. It seemed he had died the previous night, in the early hours. Brian's doctor, Norman Cowan, was our doctor too. He was the person who had broken down the door to Brian's room and discovered him lying there.

I am still convinced that Brian did not intend to take his own life. If he had, I think he would have done it with more of a flourish. As it was, he went out not with a bang but with a whimper. Brian was a showman. Had he designed his own death, it would not have been done in that timid, hole-in-the-corner way.

It was true that his life had been getting more and more bizarre, and that he had not really been in the bosom of the Beatles any more, as he had once been. He had always loved babying the Beatles, but they had grown up very quickly, as babies will. It was also true that he had too many irons in too many fires, that his empire was a bit over-stretched. But suicide? That did not ring true.

He had attempted suicide before, but he had always made sure the attempt failed, and that the note asking for help was placed where it could not be missed by anyone. But it was obvious that he had, as usual, been taking drugs that night. He was always taking pills – uppers to get him going, barbiturates to get him off to sleep. It seemed that he had been drinking, too, which was unusual for him.

I think that when he got in that night he was tired, and took a couple of sleeping-pills. Then he woke up in the middle of the night and thought, 'I must get some more sleep before the morning,' and popped in a couple more. However it happened, he did not wake up. The inquest recorded an open verdict.

When the Beatles heard the news they came straight back from Wales. They were very shocked. 'Eppy', the Eppy who had always looked after them, who had cared for them in the wild roller-coaster ride of their success, was dead. They no longer had a leader.

We all went to the funeral. I remember the Beatles coming into the synagogue, their faces white and pinched still with shock. Out of respect for Brian, they were all wearing yarmulkes. They had all washed their hair for the occasion, and the little round caps kept slipping off, falling to the floor. Wendy Hanson, who was standing behind the Beatles, had to keep picking their yarmulkes up and fixing them back on to their mop-tops. Somehow, that made me feel so sad; sadder than anything.

When Judy and I arrived back at our London flat there was a poignant reminder of Brian awaiting us. He had been delighted to hear of our daughter's safe birth and with typical generosity had sent Judy a really huge bouquet of flowers. When he had received no reply from our flat, the messenger had simply left the flowers on the doorstep. Now, like Brian, they were dead.

Brian's death really was the end of an era. *Sgt. Pepper* had been our best work to date, the most thoughtful, among the best musically, and the most successful. Brian had steered them from the dark early days of struggle and hardship to this triumph. It was Brian's absolute, unwavering conviction that the Beatles were going to be great that had swayed me when we first met, swayed me into making the crucial decision to see them perform live.

I laughed at him, on first meeting, because what he played me on the demonstration tape was not very good. I laughed, but his faith in them never wavered. He was in love with them.

So was I.

I know I've been very lucky. I've been privileged to work with some of the best composers and writers, musicians and arrangers, singers and actors in the world. The really good ones gave of themselves unstintingly and without fuss.

But of them all, none even begins to match up to the genius of those teenagers I met over thirty years ago.

They really were fab.

In my life, I've loved them all.

CODA

Pepperabilia,
or take it with a pinch of salt

Pepper was the longest series of recording sessions we had ever completed, a marathon run that was a complete departure for us. According to Geoff Emerick's calculation, we spent no fewer than 700 hours, or twenty-nine complete days, of our lives working on it in the studio. The *Please Please Me* album took 585 minutes to record.

Sgt. Pepper won the 1967 Grammy award (presented to Geoff Emerick) for best-engineered record.

Paul suggested at one time that the Beatles pose in Salvation Army uniforms for the cover photograph, an idea that was swiftly vetoed by everyone else.

It was the Beatles' eighth album in five years, and it will be the one by which they are best remembered.

Brian Epstein was against the 'group photograph' idea for the cover, so when, on the flight home to London from New York, he had a premonition that he was going to die he left a note which read simply, 'Brown paper jackets for "Sgt. Pepper's Lonely Hearts Club Band"'.

Pepper was originally going to be a double album, but the Beatles realized that there would be insufficient new material ready in time, so the spare sleeve had to be filled up with the cardboard cut-out memorabilia.

Twelve *Sgt. Pepper* promotional 'picture fridges' were made, with the album's cover photograph imprinted into the metal of their doors. At least one of these refrigerators is rumoured to be at large somewhere in the UK.

Neil Aspinall still works with the Beatles as Chairman of the Apple Corps Ltd, looking after the million and one things that affect the Beatles throughout the world every day. I reckon he has worked for them full-time and been their mate longer than anyone else.

The *Sgt. Pepper* cover features the first-ever mention of 'the Apple'.

George and Paul are wearing their MBEs on their *Pepper* uniforms.

Pirate station Radio London claimed a 'Beatles world exclusive', broadcasting a completed version of the album at 5 p.m. on 12 May 1967.

More dogs have listened to *Sgt. Pepper* than to any other album in the history of pop music.

Pepper cost about £25,000 to make – a fortune in 1967.

In 1978 Robert Stigwood produced a $12 million film version of *Sgt. Pepper*, starring the Bee Gees, Peter Frampton, Steve Martin, and Frankie Howerd. While the movie was not the success that Stigwood's *Saturday Night Fever* and *Grease* had been, the sound-track sold many millions of copies.

The badge Paul is sporting on his left sleeve for the cover photographs had the initials 'O.P.P.' on it. In the photograph it looked like O.P.D., and this was taken to mean 'Officially Pronounced Dead' by the Paul-is-dead brigade. In fact, the initials stand for 'Ontario Police Precinct'. Someone gave Paul the badge when the Beatles were in Toronto, on 17 August 1965.

One of the police detail guarding the group on that occasion was a certain . . . Sergeant Pepper!

INDEX

Abbey Road (album), 97, 139–40, 159
Abbey Road Studios,
    Beatles' off-hand approach to, 107
    besieged by fans, 108–9
    Harrison on, 14–15
    sixties technology, 22
Addy, Malcolm, 107
albums,
    Beatles' sequence of, 77–8
    concept, 67
    songs unperformable on stage, 82,
        157
'All Together Now' (song), 162
'All You Need Is Love' (song),
    159–60, 162
Ardmore & Beechwood (music
    publishers), 28
Asher family, 80
Asian Music Circle, 125
Aspinall, Neil, 8, 19, 64, 147, 168
Associated Independent Recording
    (AIR), 32
Astaire, Fred, 119

'Baby You're A Rich Man' (song), 47
'Bad Finger Boogie' (song), 141
Balzac, Honoré de, 51
Barrow, Tony, 8
BBC,
    banning of 'A Day In The Life', 4,
        155–6
    Our World programme, 159–60
    Radiophonics Workshop, 83
Beach Boys, 1, 48–9, 76
Beatlemania, 11–12, 68–9
Beatles, The (group),
    albums
        recording programme, 25
        sequence of, 77–8
    audition and recording contract
        with Martin, 27–33

Beatlemania and fame, 11–12,
    68–9
charm of, 31
comparisons with classical
    musicians, 98, 137, 154–5
concert tours
    decision to stop, 11
    Hamburg, 7
    Manila, Philippines, 7–8
    pressures of life, 10–11
    safety precautions, 9–10, 11
    San Francisco, 158–9
    Tokyo, 7
demo tape, 30
disintegration, signs of, 125
fans
    besieging studios, 108–9
    screaming at concerts, 10
high point in careers, 159
MBEs, 168
musicianship
    contrapuntal writing, 48–9
    creative rivalry, 70
    fame obscuring, 10
    free association of ideas, 138–9
    harmony, 32
    identifiable sounds, 76
    lack of formal training, 56
    learning ability, 68–9
    rock 'n' roll adapted, 44–5
    Schubert analogy, 98, 137
    twelve-bar blues form, 40, 41–2,
        47
myths surrounding, 20, 158–9
number one hits, 26–7
pressure of appearances, 6
relationships between members,
    69–70, 123–4
typical working day, 100–101
see also members by name
Beatles ('White' Album), 159

'Because' (song), 140
Bee Gees (group), 168
'Being For The Benefit Of Mr. Kite'
    (song),
  circus effects, 90–93
  idea for song, 89
  inventiveness, 76
  organ sounds, 93
  place in album, 149
  recording, 92
Bennett, Alan, 65
Berry, Chuck, 32, 44–5, 116
Best, Pete, 143
'Beyond the Fringe' (satirical revue),
    65
Bicknell, Alf, 8
Black, Cilla, 133
Black Dyke Mills Band, 64
Blake, Peter, 112, 114–16
blues music, 39–40, 42–4, 47
Boult, Sir Adrian, 84
Boyd, Pattie, 71
Brando, Marlon, 119
Brennell tape recorders, 80
Bromberg, Sheila, 135
Brown, Peter, 120
Browne, Tara, 50
Burns, Robert, 35
Burtonwood, RAF, 41–2

CBS records, 29
Cage, John, 79, 139
calliopes (steam organs), 90–92
'Can't Buy Me Love' (song), 40–41
Capitol Records, 150
Carnaby Street, 5
Cathode, Ray, 83
charts, 26–7, 151
classical music, 136–7
Cleave, Maureen, 8–9
Clifton Nurseries, Maida Vale, 117
Coleman, Ray, 51
Coleman, Syd, 28
Collins, Phil, 67, 146, 154
Columbia records, 27, 29, 30
'Come Together' (song), 97, 139
concept albums, 67
Cook, Peter, 65
Cooper, Adam, 117

Cooper, Michael, 120
Costello, Elvis, 38
cover, see Sgt. Pepper's Lonely Hearts
    Club Band (album)
Cowan, Dr Norman, 111, 163
Cribbins, Bernard, 30

Daily Express, 120
Daily Mail, 156
Daltry, Roger, 38
Dankworth, Johnny, 44
Davies, Hunter, 107
'Day In The Life, A' (song),
  banned by BBC, 4, 155–6
  ending, 61, 149
  lyrics, 50–51
  place in album, 149
  recording techniques used, 59–60
  symphony orchestra, 55–7
  tracking, 52–4
'Day Tripper' (song), 26, 82, 98
Decca records, 27–8
Deedes, Sir William (later Lord
    Deedes), 157
Diddley, Bo, 45
dilrubas, 125, 129
Domino, Fats, 45
Doors, The (group), 1
Doran, Terry, 19, 50
Dors, Diana, 116, 117
Double Fantasy (album), 140
Drake, Charlie, 30
drugs,
  BBC banning 'A Day In The Life',
    4, 155–6
  Beatles' use of, 109–11
  Sgt. Pepper: alleged references to, 2,
    52, 104, 116–17, 155–7
Dylan, Bob, 1, 39, 51, 98

EMI records, 27–8, 32
'Eleanor Rigby' (song), 26, 64, 82,
    136
electric guitar, 40
Embassy records, 27
Emerick, Geoff, 19, 53, 58, 78–82,
    86–7, 91–2, 107–8, 145, 147
Ephgrave, Joe, 116
Epstein, Brian,

Christmas single 1966, concern
  over, 25–7
concern for well-being of Beatles,
  9–10
death, 162–4
illnesses, 11, 164
listen-in for critics, 151–2
losing control of The Beatles, 6,
  164
management style, 6
overworking Beatles, 10–11
promoting early Beatles music,
  27–30
recording contract negotiated,
  27–33
Sgt. Pepper
  reaction to proposal, 6–7
Sgt. Pepper cover
  copyright problems, 118–20
  views on design, 167
Estes, John, 39, 41
Evans, Allen, 153
Evans, Mal, 8, 19, 53–4, 61, 64, 91,
  123
Evening Standard, 9
Everly Brothers, 32

Façade (Walton/Sitwell), 154–5
Faithfull, Marianne, 58
films,
  makers, 5
  profits, 67
  of *Sgt. Pepper*, 168
'Fixing A Hole' (song),
  circus effects, 89–93
  drug references alleged, 156
  McCartney's ideas on, 85
  place in album, 149
  recording process, 86–7, 92–4
Fool, The (designers), 58, 114
Frampton, Peter, 168
Fraser, Robert, 114–16
Freed, Alan, 44

Gadd, Steve, 144
'Getting Better' (song),
  idea for, 107
  lyrics, 111–12
  place in album, 149

recording, 107–8
Ginsberg, Alan, 155
'God Only Knows' (song), 48
Goldstein, Richard, 155
'Good Morning, Good Morning'
  (song), 26
  chicken noise, 75
  mixing, 75–6
  musical form, 73–4
  place in album, 149
Gorcey, Leo, 119
Grainer, Ron, 83
Grammy award, 167
groups of the sixties, 5
Gruenberg, Erich, 58–9, 128

HMV records, 27–9
Hamburg, 7, 11
Hammond organ, 101–2
Handl, Irene, 84
Hanson, Wendy, 118–20, 164
Hard Day's Night, A (album), 160
'Hard Day's Night, A' (song), 145
harmonica, 43
Harries, Dave, 19
Harris, Rolf, 30
Harrison, George,
  character, 131
  marriage, 71
  musicianship
    Indian music, 20, 47–8, 79, 124,
    130
    song-writing, 123–4
    sounds contributing to mood,
    104
  on
    Abbey Road, 14–15
    Indian music, 126–7
    recording techniques, 93–94
    Sgt. Pepper, 129–30
    sixties, 5
    'Third Man' of group, 123
Harrison, Pattie, 58
Haworth, Jann, 114–17, 120, 158
'Help' (song), 136
'Helter Skelter' (song), 137
Hendrix, Jimi, 1, 40
hippy movement, 1–2
Hitler, Adolf, 115, 118

Holly, Buddy, 45
'House Of The Rising Sun', 5
How I Won the War (film), 14
Howerd, Frankie, 168
Howlett, Kevin, 69*n*
Humperdinck, Englebert, 26
Hutton, Jack, 152

'I Am The Walrus' (song), 138–9
'(I Can't Get No) Satisfaction'
    (song), 5
'I Feel Fine' (song), 82, 87
'I Wanna Be Your Man' (song), 82
Ibbetson, Adrian, 86
In His Own Write (Lennon), 51–2
'In My Life' (song), 70
Indian influence,
    folk music, 126
    Maharishi, 123, 130
    music and instruments, 20, 47–8,
        79, 124–6
    transcendental meditation, 130–31
    Vedic literature, 126, 127–8, 131
instrumental accompaniments,
    20–21, 35, 56–8, 66–7, 134–5
instruments used,
    bass guitar, 85
    calliope (steam organ), 90–93
    dilrubas, 125, 129
    electric guitar, 40
    harmonica, 43
    harmonium, 91–2
    harpsichord, 85
    Lowry organ, 101–2
    mellotron, 16, 18, 20, 23
    pianette, 108
    sitar, 20, 125
    swordmandel, 20, 126
    tabla, 126, 129
    tamboura drones, 79, 108, 126,
        129
'It's Only A Northern Song' (song),
    124
Ives, Burl, 75

Jagger, Mick, 1, 58
Jefferson, Blind Lemon, 40–41
Jesus Christ,
    Lennon's gaffe, 9, 11–12

proposed as figure on cover, 115
Jewell, Derek, 153
John, Elton, 38
Jones, Brian, 58
Jones, Tom, 72
Joplin, Janice, 11

Kaempfert, Bert, 33
King, Tony, 69
King Lear (Shakespeare), 139
King record label, 43–5
Kinks, The (group), 5
Knowle Park, Kent, 89
Koger, Marijke, 58, 114
Kroll, Jack, 154–5

L'après-midi d'un faune (Debussy), 84
Lawrence, T. E, 116
Leander, Mike, 134
Lennon, Cynthia, 72, 78
Lennon, John,
    appearance, 152
    art training, 39, 41
    attention span, 99
    drug use, 109–11
    involvement in recording process,
        22–3
    'Jesus Christ' gaffe, 9, 11–12
    lyric writing, 50–52, 77–8
    McCartney, relationship with, 110
    musicianship
        bass guitarist, 47
        harmonica, love of, 43
        lack of blues influence, 47
        McCartney's influence, 98
        song writing, 71, 89, 103,
            137–9
        voice, 13, 32, 53, 97
    on
        classical musicians, 74–5
        Epstein's death, 162
        his songs, 24
        Martin, 69
        old age, 36
        rock 'n' roll, 51
    technique of recording, interest in,
        61–2
    Weybridge home, 71–3
    Yoko Ono's influence, 66, 73, 140

Let It Be (album), 159
Lewis, Jerry Lee, 45
Lewisohn, Mark, 36, 69*n*, 154
'Like A Rolling Stone' (song), 5
Liston, Sonny, 116
'Little Help From My Friends, A'
    (song),
  'Billy Shears' character, 141–43
  place in album, 149
  recording, 142
  Starr's singing, 141–43
Little Richard, 45
Littleton, Humphrey, 44
Liverpool, 41–2
Livingston, Alan, 150
Lockhart Smith, Judy, *see* Martin,
    Judy
Lockwood, Sir Joseph, 118
'Love Me Do' (song), 30, 43–4, 143
'Lovely Rita' (song),
  idea for song, 64
  place in album, 149
  recording, 95–6
Lowry organ, 101–2
'Lucy In The Sky With Diamonds'
    (song),
  drug associations, 104
  lyrics, 103–4
  musical form, 102
  place in album, 149
  recording, 101
Lush, Richard, 66, 107
lyrics,
  Lennon's, 50–52, 77–8
  messages in, 77–8
  see also songs by name

McBain, Angus, 121
McCallum, David, 58
McCartney, Jim, 34
McCartney, Linda, 38
McCartney, Paul,
  appearance, 152
  artistic interests, 114
  cover of *Sgt. Pepper*, 113
  Lennon, relationship with, 110
  life style, 71
  musicianship
    arranging skills, 35–6

  avant-garde interests, 79–80
  bass guitarist, 85
  counterpoint, 136
  lateral thinking, 99
  Lennon's influence, 98
  most talented Beatle, 86, 137
  piano-playing, 53–4
  song writing techniques, 34, 80,
    87–8, 136–7, 139–40
  voice, 35, 66
  myth of his death, 20, 158–9
  on
    albums, 133
    'Lovely Rita', 97
    moustaches, 121–2
    music papers, 111
    song-writing, 95
    touring, 10–11
    Yoko Ono, 73
McGhee, Brownie, 43
MacKenzie, Henry, 35
Magical Mystery Tour (album), 159
'Magical Mystery Tour' (song), 162
Maharishi,
  Beatles' visit
    to India, 130
    to Wales, 162
  influence on Beatles, 123
Mann, William, 152
Marcos, Ferdinand *and* Imelda, 7–8
Mardas, Alex, 62
Martin, George,
  collaborator rather than boss, 84
  experimental recording techniques,
    48, 83
  family
    father's death, 160–61
    Judy, *see* Martin, Judy
    Lucie, 162
  first meeting with Epstein, 28–32
  keyboard player, 85
  musical arrangements, approach to,
    20–21, 35, 56–8, 66–7, 134–5
  musical influence, 48
  Parlophone records and, 28–9, 45
  Ray Cathode, as, 83
  specialities, 78
  studio relations with Beatles, 68–9
  work load, 37–8

Martin, Judy, 11, 32, 52, 72, 160, 162
Martin, Steve, 168
Mellers, Wilfred, 153–4
mellotron, 16, 18, 20, 23
Melody Maker (magazine), 26, 152
Miller, Jonathan, 65
Milligan, Spike, 93
Moog, Robert, 108
Moore, Dudley, 65
Motown, Tamla, 1
music papers, 26–7, 111, 152–5
'My Generation' (song), 5

Nash, Graham, 58
New Musical Express (magazine), 26–7, 153
New Statesman, 153–4
New York Village Voice, 155
Nicol, Jimmy, 107
'Norwegian Wood' (song), 78, 124
Novachord, 102–3

'Octopus's Garden' (song), 139
Ono, Yoko, 66, 73, 140
Orbison, Roy, 45
outtakes, 19

Paramor, Norrie, 30, 107
Parlophone record label,
    Martin's role, 27–9
    profits for EMI, 32
Parnell, Jack, 44
'Penny Lane' (song), 14, 26, 70
    issued as single, 26–7, 34, 89, 150
Perkins, Carl, 45
Pet Sounds (album), 48–9
Phillips records, 28
pianettes, 108
Picasso, Pablo, 23
Please Please Me (album), 77, 121
'Please Please Me' (song), 26, 30
Portmeirion, North Wales, 11
Posthuma, Simon, 58, 114
Presley, Elvis, 29, 32, 40, 45, 48, 53, 63
Preuss, Oscar, 29
Procol Harum (group), 5
profits of record industry, 67–8

Puttnam, David, 119
Pye records, 27

Quant, Mary, 5, 131

radio of the sixties, 5
Radiophonics Workshop, 83
'Rain' (song), 78–9
Randall, Freddy, 44
Record Mirror, 26
recording techniques,
    ambiophony system, 59
    Artificial Double Tracking (ADT), 82
    echo, 53
    experimental, 48
    frequency changer, 22, 46
    Lennon's interest in, 61–2
    Leslie loudspeakers, 81, 105
    mixing, 21–2, 105
    overdubbing, 21
    sixties' technology, 22
    tape recorders
        limitations of, 80–81
        speeds, 91–2, 96–7
    volume production, 45–7
Reed, Lou, 98
Regal Zonophone records, 29
Regent Sound studio, 86–7
Reidy, Frank, 35
'Release Me' (song), 26
Revolver (album), 25, 69, 76, 77–9, 82, 159
Richard, Cliff, 19, 30, 72, 107
Robinson, Smokey, 45
rock 'n' roll music, 1, 39–40, 44–5, 51, 139
Rolling Stones, The, 5, 40, 44, 76, 120
Rubber Soul (album), 76, 77, 159

San Francisco, 158–9
Sellers, Peter, 83–4, 125
Sgt. Pepper's Lonely Hearts Club Band (album)
    catalogue of Beatles' skills, 76–7
    contemporary art, as, 137
    cover
        copyright problems, 117–20

design team, 113–16
Epstein's views, 167
figures included, 115–17
importance of, 64
lettering, 116
lyrics printed on, 4
McCartney, on, 112
McCartney's badge, 168
'marijuana plants', 116
moustaches, 121–2
myths surrounding, 20, 158–9
uniforms, 120
drugs, claimed allusions to, 2, 52,
   104, 116–17, 155–7
editing, 150
epitomizing sixties, 157
film versions, 168
lyrics
   interpretation of their message,
   2–3
   mysticism in, 3–4
number one in charts, 151
production costs, 168
reaction to
   expressing sixties mood, 4–5
   Grammy award, 167
   pop music changed, 1–2
   rapturous critics, 151–5
   USA, 154–5
release, 1–2, 151–5
restraint of, 131–2
revolutionary album, 64–5
running order of songs, 148–50
sales, 151
spare sleeve's memorabilia, 167
time spent recording, 167
Ultra High Quality Recording
   edition, 61
unperformable on stage, 82, 157
see also songs by name
'Sgt. Pepper's Lonely Hearts Club
   Band' (song),
inspiration for, 63–4
live performance, illusion of, 65,
   76–7
musical arrangements, 66–7
recording techniques, 65–6
reprise, 147–8
Shand, Jimmy, 118

'She Loves You' (song), 76, 158
'She's Leaving Home' (song),
   classical accompaniment, 76
   contrapuntal harmonies, 48, 136
   McCartney solo, 125
   place in album, 148–9
   recording, 135–6
Simone, Nina, 43
Sinatra, Frank, 156, 157–8
sitars, 20, 125
Smith, Norman 'Hurricane', 145
'Something' (song), 139
Sounds Incorporated (group), 74
South Bank Show (TV show), 5,
   10–11, 15, 50, 55, 63, 64, 67,
   70, 94, 95, 97, 110, 111, 112,
   117, 121, 127, 131, 133, 143,
   145, 146, 160
Stanfield, Lisa, 38
Starkey, Richard, *see* Starr, Ringo
Starr, Ringo,
   home life, 71
   illness, 107
   musicianship
      drumming technique, 21, 55, 74,
      143–5
      voice, 142
   on
      drug use, 110
      making *Sgt. Pepper*, 100, 160
      Martin, 69
   one-liners, 145–6
   'replacement man' of group, 143
   on touring, 10
   'With A Little Help From My
      Friends', 141
Stigwood, Robert, 168
Stockhausen, Karlheinz, 79
'Strawberry Fields Forever'
   composition
      form, 16
      Lennon's nostalgia, 13–14
      lyrics, 15, 17
      melody, 15–16
   Indian instruments, 20
   issued as single, 26–7, 34, 89, 150
   musical arrangement, 16–20
   recording, 16–23
Sunday Times, 113, 153

Sutcliffe, Stuart, 85
swordmandel (Indian harp), 20, 126

tablas, 126, 129
tamboura drones, 79–80, 108, 126, 129
tape recorders, 80–81, 91–2, 96–7
Terry, Sonny, 43
theatre of the sixties, 5
Tibetan Book of the Dead (Leary ed.), 79
'Time Beat/Waltz In Orbit' (electronic sounds record), 83
Times, The, 98, 152
'Tomorrow Never Knows' (song), 60, 76, 79–82, 158
Townsend, Ken, 22, 58, 82, 107, 148
transcendental meditation, 130–31, *see also* Maharishi
Tug of War (album), 144

United States of America,
    cover-cult, 113
    critical reviews, 154–5
    rock 'n' roll recording artists, 44–5
    sales, 150, 151
    tours
        Chicago, 9
        Denver, 9
        San Francisco, 158–9
    unpopularity after Lennon's gaffe, 9

Voormann, Klaus, 124

Ward, Christopher, 122
'We Can Work It Out' (song), 26
Webber, Sir Andrew Lloyd, 98
Weissmuller, Johnny, 119
West, Mae, 120
'When I'm Sixty-Four' (song), 26, 34–8
White, Andy, 143
'Whiter Shade Of Pale, A' (song), 5
Who, The, 1, 5
Willis, Ted (later Lord Willis), 157
Wilson, Brian, 48–9
Winner, Langdon, 154
'Within You Without You' (song),
    Indian influence, 77, 124–6
    lyrics, 124–5
    musical form, 158
    recording, 126–9

Yardbirds The, 40
Yellow Submarine (album), 124
'Yellow Submarine' (song), 26
'Yesterday' (song), 47, 70, 76, 125, 134
'You Never Give Me Your Money' (song), 140
'Your Mother Should Know' (song), 162